Memories of Inlet

Letty Kirch Haynes

North Country Books, Inc.
Utica, New York

Memories of Inlet

Design by Zach Steffen & Rob Igoe Jr.

Hardcover ISBN 1-59531-009-6
Paperback ISBN 1-59531-010-X

Library of Congress Cataloging-in-Publication Data

Haynes, Letty Kirch.
  Memories of Inlet / Letty Kirch Haynes.
      p. cm.
   ISBN 1-59531-009-6 (alk. paper) -- ISBN 1-59531-010-X (alk. paper)
   1. Inlet (N.Y.)--History--Anecdotes. 2. Inlet (N.Y.)--Social life and customs--Anecdotes. 3.
Inlet (N.Y.)--Biography--Anecdotes. 4. Historic buildings--New York (State)--Inlet. 5. Inlet
(N.Y.)--Buildings, structures, etc. I. Title.
   F129.I44H39 2006
   974.7'52--dc22
                                            2006013141

North Country Books, Inc.
311 Turner Street
Utica, New York 13501
ncbooks@adelphia.net
www.northcountrybooks.com

Dedicated, with love, to "Red"

Contents

Acknowledgements...vii

Preface...ix

1   Early Hotels...1

2   Steamboats...27

3   Children's Camps...33

4   Buildings and Businesses.................................41

5   Recreation..61

6   Public Services..73

7   Roads..83

8   Private Residences...89

9   Personal Reminiscences..................................99

Appendix A 1900 Census & 1910 Census.........................125

Appendix B Elected Officials....................................137

Appendix C Hamilton County Veterans.........................139

Appendix D Minutes of the First Town Board Meeting.....140

Acknowledgements

Without the suggestion of Kris Condie, I probably would never have started writing this book. She, Mary Lee Kalil, and Joanne Vogan had already collected much information. Inez Rudd and Barbara Wermuth have extensive postcard and picture collections which they generously shared and allowed me to copy. The Old Forge Historical Society was a valuable source of information, as were old newspaper clippings I had saved. Perhaps of greatest importance is the fact that I am descended on both sides of my family from early settlers, which gave me access to personal memories, stories, and diaries from those early days of Inlet.

This short book does not in any way pretend to be a complete history. My family's years have been spent on the south side of town, so I am naturally more familiar with events which took place there. My apologies to the Sixth and Seventh Lakers and those on Limekiln Lake who may feel somewhat neglected.

Some of the information proved confusing, as different sources did not always agree. I tried, in these cases, to use what seemed most generally accepted. Because of the vast amount of material that could have been included, I chose to limit this particular book of memories mostly to the years before World War II.

Many thanks go to Ruth Blynt for her countless hours of help with editing. Finally I must acknowledge David, Russ, and Debbie Haynes, who spent infinite time and demonstrated endless patience helping me learn enough of the intricacies of a computer to enable me to write this book.

Looking up the inlet towards Fourth Lake

Preface

Flowing through the southwest corner of the Adirondack Park, a six million acre tract of land protected by New York State, are eight connecting lakes called the Fulton Chain. Originally but a series of streams and rivers, a dam built in about 1798, in what is now Old Forge, turned this area into the beautiful lakes we enjoy today. The Fulton Chain name came from Robert Fulton, who was commissioned in 1811 to explore the possibility of using these lakes as a passage from the Hudson River to the Great Lakes.

Nestled 1,818 feet above sea level, at the head of Fourth Lake and along the shore of the channel into tiny Fifth Lake, lies the community of Inlet. Appropriately called "Mountain Village of Beautiful Lakes," Inlet is surrounded by Adirondack mountain peaks and looks down the expanse of Fourth Lake to spectacular sunsets at the western end.

Formerly part of the Town of Morehouse, the area was established as the Town of Inlet in January 1902 by a committee of three—Frank E. Tiffany, C. R. Jones, and Charles A. O'Hara. The first town meeting was held on January 14, 1902, at O'Hara's hotel. With 35 votes cast, all by men (women did not yet have the right to vote), Frank Tiffany was elected supervisor; Charles O'Hara, town clerk; John Cassidy, Raymond Norton, and Christopher Van Arnam, justices of the peace; and Austin Dobson and Wellington Kenwell, assessors. Also chosen were Fred Kirch, W. Kenwell, and R.G. Wallace, commissioners of highways; Peter Burr, tax collector; William Wilkinson and Frank Stahl, constables; and Abner Blakeman, game constable.

Early Hotels

The 1905 census, representing the first for the new village of Inlet, showed a total population of 168 people, living in thirty-seven houses or in one of the town's six hotels: The Arrowhead, Hess Camp, Cedar Island House, Neodak, Rocky Point Inn, and Seventh Lake House. Fred Kirch, who ran the steamboat, seems to have escaped the census taker.

The beauty of the area was beginning to attract a different type of tourist, and fishermen and hunters were giving way to people in search of other forms of recreation and relaxation. With these visitors came the need for more comfortable lodging, which gave growth to the many beautiful hotels that were to grace the shores of the lakes for many years.

Probably the first place in the Inlet area to accommodate paying guests was Cedar Island Camp, located on the three islands collectively referred to as Cedar Island, totaling about five acres. Fred Hess, one of the earliest settlers in the area, built a rustic cabin there sometime in the 1870s. Originally built to house an ailing friend, the cabin was in the direct path of oncoming sportsmen and soon became a popular stopover point. Around 1885, Fred Kirch came to the area, and during his first winter, as a young lad of thirteen, was hired to stay on Cedar Island to prevent it from reverting to the state from the "squatters" who had claimed it. The "squatter"

Cedar Island Camp

was probably Fred Hess. As an increasing number of sportsmen sought lodging at Cedar Island Camp, Hess enlarged the original building and added others.

In 1895, Hess sold Cedar Island to Joseph Porter and moved to Inlet, where he opened the first true hotel in the area at the head of Fourth Lake, the site later occupied by the Arrowhead Hotel.

Hess's new establishment was called The Inlet Inn and acommodated twenty people. In 1899, he sold it to Charles O'Hara. It was here that the first town election was held, for which O'Hara was paid $24.00.

Hess then built another hotel nearer the waterfront which he named the Hess House. This was also quite small and was covered with bark siding.

He soon enlarged it, and it was sometimes called Arrowhead House. After a fire destroyed this structure in 1913, O'Hara built the beautiful new Arrowhead.

Charles O'Hara had begun his business by opening a barbershop which he enlarged to include a store. When he became the owner of the lovely new Arrowhead, his advertisement warned:

> The management makes it a rule to find accommodations for desirable guests only. We refuse all having pulmonary troubles. The patronage of all objectionable persons is declined, and we offer an exclusive and desirable summer home. Hebrew patronage is not accepted.

Fred Hess

The Inlet Inn

The cost for accommodations in O'Hara's hotel was three dollars a day.

The Arrowhead, with its yellow and green structure, boathouse with an upper deck that faced the channel, and long dock where steamboats rested, was an imposing landmark for many years. It was to become the generally accepted polling place for elections and town meetings. It also hosted several famous guests, including Charles Evans Hughes, statesman and governor of New York, and Fanny Hurst, a famous writer of the time.

Interior of The Inlet Inn

Hess House

However, the event which was to give the Arrowhead its most lasting fame occurred after a young man by the name of Chester Gillette registered there on a day in 1906. He had come to the Adirondacks with his pregnant girlfriend, Grace Brown, allegedly to marry her. Gillette rented a boat from the Glenmore Hotel on nearby Big Moose Lake and took Brown rowing. When the boat was not returned, searchers found it floating upside down and later discovered Brown's body on the bottom of the lake. A subsequent search for Gillette found him nonchalantly enjoying his vacation at the Arrowhead, which is where he was arrested. Gillette was eventually tried for the murder of

THE LEGENDARY FRED HESS, who carved Inlet out of a wilderness, would rather hunt than run his hotels. He is shown in this old picture bringing back a trophy of the chase to Cedar Isle.

"The Legendary Fred Hess"

Grace Brown, and he became the first person to die in the electric chair at Auburn State Prison. These tragic events have been retold in several books and movies, keeping the couple's memory alive and giving the hotel a certain amount of dubious fame.

In 1962, the Town of Inlet bought the Arrowhead property, intending to have the old building razed. This caused one of the town's many altercations. The contract was let to the lowest bidder who was willing to tear down the hotel instead of burning it. But before that could happen, the building mysteriously caught on fire and burned to the ground, and many bitter feelings ensued. The land was then turned into a much needed public park, and a new building was constructed to house the town offices and meeting rooms.

Hotel owner Fred Hess, having sold first Cedar Island and then his Hess House, built yet another hotel in 1894. This one he named Hess Camp. Built on what is probably the most beautiful spot in Inlet, on a hill at the head of Fourth Lake, the site commands a magnificent view. In 1905, Hess Camp was run by C. Edward Duquette. Tragedy struck on the night of October 24, 1905, when the lights went off in the hotel. Duquette took a lantern to the gas house which supplied the hotel's power to find out what had happened. Unbeknownst to him, acetylene gas was leaking from the tanks and had filled the service building. When the unfortunate

New Arrowhead

Hess Camp

Duquette opened the door, his lantern ignited the gas, causing an explosion which threw him twenty feet and ripped the clothes from his body. His hair was burned to a crisp, and every bone in his body was crushed. Nothing could be done to save Duquette, and he died a short time later.

At this time the Wellington Kenwells took over Hess Camp. By 1915, an enlarged building was in the hands of Philo Wood, who renamed it the Wood Hotel. That name remained, though Wood later sold the hotel to the Dunay family, who retained ownership until the hotel closed. The building still stands, unused and derelict, a shadow of its former beauty and a poignant reminder of an era when gracious vacationing in hotels was a way of life.

Another early Inlet hotel was the Neodak, built by the Pratt family around 1900 and taken over by William Preston in 1905. Situated on the south shore of Fourth Lake just a short distance

Wood Hotel

from town, the Neodak was a small frame building with enough room for the family and a handful of guests. Sometime around 1910, the hotel's former porter, a man by the name of Roy Rogers, became its new owner. With his wife Emma, he operated the small hotel until the summer of 1919, when it caught fire one Sunday morning. Church services were let out in order to form a bucket brigade, but despite these efforts, the hotel burned to the ground.

Not to be discouraged, the Rogers rebuilt a much larger structure, and in 1920, the New Neodak was open for business.

In a brochure printed about this time, Rogers boasts:

> The old Neodak was considerably smaller—we can take care of 100 and more guests at a time. All these rooms are lighted by electricity, they have access to hot and cold running water and bath. The steamers of the Fulton Navigation Company stop at our dock daily.

He further exclaims:

> Not necessary to walk a mile or so for a one-step or a fox-trot. Casino over water.

And regarding the cooking:

> Mrs. Rogers has general charge of it, and Mrs. Rogers knows how. Home cooking, the best of vegetables from our own big garden, fresh meats delivered at our landing daily, eggs from our own hens, and the very best in milk...that gives you an idea of what the New Neodak table is like.

Though abhorrent to us today, Rogers echoes the antisemitic policy of many hotels at the time by including the reassurance that "We have never entertained Hebrews." The cost for all these amenities during the prime season was twenty-five dollars per week.

Of course, the problem Rogers occasionally had with his water was not mentioned in this brochure. The supply line ran through the shallow channel connecting Fifth and Fourth Lakes, and upon more than one occasion, someone on a dare, or perhaps for spite, would cut the line. Woe to the ears of those within listening distance when this was discovered by Roy.

For nearly forty years the Neodak would be run by the Rogers family, first by Roy and Emma, then by their son John, and finally by their daughter, Ella Moran. As the older generation with its traditions gave way to the younger, so did activities and ways of entertainment change. It became the custom at the Neodak that once a week, with car horns blowing, guests would parade to the Sixth Lake Dam, where the tour boat Osprey would convey them up the lake to a steak roast. Ella has explained that after dinner, guests gathered at a large tree for the "Chief Neodakus" ceremony. Chief Neodakus was an imaginary Native American who supposedly was buried under the tree. One of the men in the group would don an Indian blanket and an elaborate headdress and become the chief for the evening. He would then pick a "bride" from the young women in the group, and the couple would disappear into the woods, accompanied by whistles and catcalls.

Various developments of the Neodak

Day activities included canoe tilting and theme parties, with guests dressing like babies, shipwreck survivors, and hula dancers, depending on the theme for the day. Also very popular was the Walla Walla room at the back of the hotel, where liquid refreshment and conviviality could be had far into the night.

Picnicking was another popular pastime, and a favorite destination was Split Rock. Just a short hike through the woods across from the hotel, it is a picturesque place where a huge rock shadows a small stream.

The outbreak of World War II changed the mood at the hotel. Everyone was affected in some way, and a

Osprey boat trip
with John Rogers and guests

SPLIT ROCK NEAR INLET, CENTRAL ADIRONDACK MOUNTAINS, N. Y.

Split Rock

Neodak burning

more serious atmosphere caused the parties to lose their gaiety. Mr. Rogers became tired of the pall that was hanging over his hotel and sent a letter to Adolf Hitler, asking him to end the war because of its adverse effects on his business. When asked if he thought it would do any good, Rogers said no, but he wanted Hitler to know his feelings.

By 1959, new times and especially new building codes made renovations too costly to be worthwhile. The Neodak was offered to the town for $66,000, but the offer was rejected; so, like many of these symbols of another era, the hotel was purposely burned to the ground. Many people were attracted to the sight of this large building going up in flames. Boats collected along the shore and watchers stood all around. The pilot of a seaplane swooping over to view the spectacle became so distracted that while attempting to land, he flew into a canoe, cutting it in half. Fortunately, the occupants escaped without permanent injury—just one person suffered cuts to his leg.

After the fire, the land was auctioned off in individual lots. The sloping hill that once was graced by the Neodak Hotel is now an empty lawn, although some of the outbuildings still remain as private cottages.

Rocky Point Inn, rising out of the trees under the shadow of Rocky Mountain, was one of the distinctive landmarks on Fourth

Lake in those early years. The hotel was built on a peninsula which curved out into the lake and protected a beautiful sand beach. On the outermost end of this rocky point was a charming, rustic gazebo. Archibald Delmarsh, who managed the Cedar Island House until it burned in 1915, took over Rocky Point Inn from Longstaff, Wallace, Niles, and Parker. He, his son, and his grandson, all named Archibald, were to own it until 1987.

Rocky Point was more formal than the Neodak and catered to a more aristocratic clientele. Mary Pickford and Errol Flynn were only two of the many celebrities who stayed there. In the dining room, with its walls of windows overlooking the lake, tie and coat were the required dress for men. Meals were sumptuous and served with elegance. A putting green and immaculately cared for tennis courts indicated the choice of recreation here, along with the launches and sailboats that graced the waterfront. Rocky Point Inn was the beautiful setting for many wedding receptions and other celebrations.

Rocky Point's brochure advertised:

> The Inn, its cottages and grounds are lighted by gas, and the other facilities include steam heat, hot and cold water, baths, open fireplaces, electric bells, and sanitary plumbing. The purest water piped from a cold forest spring is used for drinking and cooking.

This was quite a change from the earlier days when tents had been the only accommodation for some guests. Prices with these new amenities ranged from $17.50 to $30.00 a week.

Unfortunately, in 1989, this hotel, too, gave way to changing economic and vacationing lifestyles, and it was demolished to make way for town houses. The stately chimneys and gabled roofs that had towered over the evergreens were no longer a landmark on the lake.

Recognizing its historical importance, the last owner, Archie Delmarsh III, composed the following account of Rocky Point Inn.

A History of Rocky Point Resort

On August 8th, 1844, Farrand Benedict and Marshall Shedd purchased a large tract of land in Hamilton County from the people of the State of New York. The land upon

The sand beach at Rocky Point   *Rocky Point Arbor*

Remodeled dining room at Rocky Point

which the Inn was built was included in this purchase. The land was used primarily for tree harvesting through a succession of owners until its sale by James Galvin to Ella L. Holiday, Emiline Crawford, and James Niles in 1892.

Operating as the Rocky Point Inn Co., they began construction of the original Inn and opened for business in the spring of 1893. James Galvin carried the mortgage on the Inn until October 8th, 1894. At that time, a new mortgage was taken with Lousia Burrell in the amount of $6,000. And the prior mortgage was paid off. This was to be the beginning of a 27-year relationship between the Burrells and the Inn.

The operation of the Inn during those early years was not successful. On January 18, 1896, the business was reorganized with the same name and same owners. However, they were eventually unable to fulfill their obligation to the mortgage holder, Burrell. On April 15th, 1904, Burrell foreclosed on the Rocky Point Inn Co. Thus ended the stewardship of Holiday, Crawford and Niles after eleven years.

From 1904–1911, Burrell leased the property to a succession of three operators who were all unsuccessful.

The first lessee was Thomas Parkes, owner of the Hotel Hamilton in New York City. He operated the Inn for only one season, 1905. His brochure says he constructed a new dining room.

During the 1906 and 1907 season Mark Wallace was the operator. From his brochure it appears his major contributions to the Inn were the construction of some wooden cottages and the addition of a gravity feed water system. Prior to the cottage construction old brochures show several raised platform tent structures on the property north of the main inn. From 1909 through 1910, the operator was H. H. Longstaff whose wife was owner / manager of the Mohawk Hotel on Fourth Lake simultaneously. Longstaff was also unable to operate the Inn profitably and at the end of the 1910 season he moved to the

Archie and Laura Delmarsh with baby Mary Jane

Mohawk to assist his wife. It was claimed, and later confirmed, by the late owner of the Mohawk, Mr. Wilcox, that Mr. Longstaff floated most of the Rocky Point furniture down the lake to the Mohawk when he left.

While Rocky Point Inn was being managed by Niles, Parkes, Wallace and Longstaff, a young couple from Greig, N.Y., Archie and Laura Delmarsh, were managing a hotel complex situated on Cedar Island in Fourth Lake and not far from Rocky Point.

Arch was a long time Adirondack resident having come to Inlet in 1886 as a sixteen-year-old. The Delmarshes

ROCKY POINT INN, 4TH LAKE.   ADIRONDACK MTS. INLET, N. Y.

Rocky Point Inn

were hard workers who had built a fine clientele on Cedar Island. The facilities and building on the island were far superior to the Rocky Point property at that time.

When the possibility of purchasing Rocky Point arose, a guest on the island was very instrumental in helping make the decision. He wrote a very foresighted letter to the Delmarshes suggesting that this new fangled thing called an automobile would make a hotel that was not on an island much more attractive in the future. He also offered to build a camp for himself (now the Damon camp) and to sell it to the Delmarshes in five years for $5,000.

With the encouragement of Stevens, the Delmarshes purchased the Inn on January 17, 1911, for $23,000. The terms were $5,000 cash down and $18,000 mortgaged at 4.2%, and $1,000 minimum due annually on principal. At the time Arch was 41 years old. He and Laura were blessed the previous September with their first child, Arch Jr., born on Cedar Island. Burrell still held the mortgage.

In a note dated 2/13/11, Burrell authorizes Arthur Rarick to deliver the keys to Delmarsh and advises that the icehouse was just filled for a cost of $46 and that Delmarsh is welcome to it.

Business was slow at first for the Delmarshes as it was for the previous operators. A letter from Burrell dated February 1st, 1916, indicates that no principal payment had been made since 1911, and is written in a very threatening way. Delmarsh replies "as you say, I have not made any payments in 5 years but have spent over $15,000 on the property." Later in the month Delmarsh gave Burrell a bank note in the amount of $1,000.

By February of 1919, the business was improving and Burrell writes Delmarsh to thank him for an interest check in the amount of $708.75 and a principal check for $2,750. In January of 1920, Delmarsh made a $3,000 principal payment. In January of 1921, an $8,000 payment and finally in February of 1921, Delmarsh makes his last payment and the mortgage is burned.

The deed Burrell to Delmarsh, interestingly is not delivered until February 1924.

Upon Arch Sr.'s death in October 1948, the property passed to his son Arch Jr. He and his wife, Norma, operated the Inn from that time until 1973. During those years many improvements were made to the Inn with the addition of a large dining room, gymnasium, and several large and small cottages.

During the '50s and into the late '60s the Inn was very successful. However, with the advent of easy air travel, air conditioning, and a penchant for people to prefer going south in the winter rather than north in the summer, business began to lag.

When Arch III and his wife, Shirley, purchased the Inn in 1972, there were few customers and much maintenance work to do. With the help of their boys and many other local people who worked for them, they were able to bring the business back and operated it successfully until 1987 when the property was sold for development.

* * *

No history of old hotels would be complete without including the only one remaining in present-day use, beautiful Holl's Inn. The property was originally purchased from the Pratt estate by Charles O'Hara, who had owned the Arrowhead Hotel at one time. In 1920, he leased the site to Mrs. Wilcox from New York City. She planned to build a riding school and camp for girls, but when it became obvious that she was unable to afford the venture, O'Hara resumed management of the property. The two stories of rooms that had been completed for Mrs. Wilcox were raised, and a lobby, dining room,

Oscar and Rosemary Holl

and kitchen were established underneath. The new hotel was named the Ara-Ho, which is O'Hara spelled backwards. Charles's brother Bernard, with his wife Mary, ran the hotel from 1923 until 1933.

According to current owner Rosemary Holl, Mary O'Hara told her that the first day she walked into the hotel, the dishwasher was drunk and the chef quit—not an auspicious beginning. Mary also told Rosemary that the Ku Klux Klan burned crosses on the front lawn of the Arrowhead because Charlie was Catholic.

In 1935, bachelor brothers Oscar and Hans Holl bought the hotel and gave it the new name Holl's Inn. Eventually Oscar married, and in 1956 Hans moved on to the Albedor. Holl's Inn has the distinction of never having had a serious fire, so the main building today looks much as it did originally. There have been extensive ground-level units added to the side, extending quite a distance along the shore, and a year-round home was built for the Holl family. Although Oscar has died, his wife Rosemary continues to open the hotel each summer. Wicker furniture from the '20s decorates the lounge, and a large stone fireplace emanates heat and cheer on chilly days. The spacious windows

THE ARA-HO HOTEL, FOURTH LAKE, INLET, CENTRAL ADIRONDACK MTS., N. Y.

Ara-Ho Hotel

along the dining room wall overlook the vista of Fourth Lake. Many of the same families return year after year, bringing their children and grandchildren.

Although much of the hired help now comes from abroad instead of being garnered from the local crop of youth, Holl's Inn is the only place left in Inlet where one can experience a semblance of the life of an old Adirondack hotel.

Anna and Hans Holl's daughter, Helen Holl Estabrook, has written "A Little About My Parents," which includes a section about the early days of the Inn.

Both of my parents, Anna and Hans, were born in southern Germany and came to this country in the 1920's. My mother, Anna Hagen, was born in Spaichingen, one of ten children, on October 30, 1901. My father, Hans Holl, one of six children, was born in Horb on December 21, 1900. Both families were very poor. My mother had to take care of her brothers and sisters until she was in her 20s, so that her parents could work their farm and produce enough food to feed their family. My father's family had a small felt factory in Horb, where they produced felt liners for the German army. These liners were for mittens and boots. At around the time that my father was fourteen years old, he and his brother, Oscar, had to leave home. There just wasn't enough food to feed their family. My father went on to various hotels in Germany and Switzerland, and as an apprentice to many famous chefs, learned the very best of culinary skills.

Hans came to this country in 1923, and from then until 1935 worked in many famous restaurants in New York City, the most famous being The Waldorf Astoria. His brother, Oscar, came to this country about the same time,

Anna Holl

and worked in many of the same hotels, learning office and management skills.

My father was a great saver of money. He never forgot arriving in America penniless. In spite of the great depression, he was one of the few people able to save enough money to have a car in New York City. It was this car that destined him to end up in Inlet, N.Y. It seems that the famous skater, Sonja Henie, a patron of The Waldorf Astoria, needed a place to practice for the 1932 World Olympics. Lake Placid was the closest place for her to do this,

and so, she hired Hans to drive her there for practices, whenever he was able to do so. As a result, he spent a lot of time in Lake Placid, and at one time seriously considered buying the St. Moritz Hotel, which was then the most affluent place to stay in Lake Placid. However, his travels with Sonja took him straight through Old Forge and Inlet. It was at that time that he discovered approximately three hundred fifty acres of land with hundreds of feet of waterfront, the Ara-Ho Hotel on the South Shore Road, owned by the O'Hara family being for sale. The area reminded him so very much of his homeland, located almost within the Black Forest, that he purchased the property with cash. (He never owned a credit card, and I'm sure there was no such thing at that time anyway.)

Back to my mother: She came to this country in 1927 and worked in New York as well. Her arrival in America was a very traumatic one. She was supposed to be met by her sponsors, but name after name was called and still she waited. Naturally, her anxiety grew as she saw herself being deserted in this strange country. Finally, the very last one left on the ship, her name was called. After raising her brothers and sisters, she was well suited to become a governess. She took care of the children whose parents owned the Tootsie Roll Foundation from the time of her arrival in this country, until she married my father on March 30, 1939.

Hans Holl on the ship

My parents only lived about 35 miles apart in Germany, but had never met. It was in a German Club in New York City that they first became acquainted. However, since they had little money, they had to save approximately twelve years before they would marry.

Helen Estabrook continues:

My father and Oscar had a great deal of work to complete before they opened Holl's Inn for business. There had been a fire on the premises before my father purchased the hotel. I believe they opened in 1936. However, my aunt, Rosemary Holl, may differ with me on that.

Woops! What happened to Anna? My father did drive back to New York City to see her, and the wedding took place immediately in Hoboken, N.J., with Oscar as one witness and a man, unknown to me, as the other witness. On the same day of the wedding, my father treated my

Chef Hans

mother to her first ride to her future home, Inlet, N.Y. Upon arrival there, she was expected to cook a meal, (a freshly killed chicken) for Daddy and Oscar.

My father, mother, and uncle worked long hours and ran a very successful resort. My father, using all of his culinary skills, managed that end of the business while Oscar, using his ability to do bookwork, ran the office and acted as a gallant host to the guests.

Woops...here I go again. Anna? Well, Daddy knew all too well what she was capable of, after raising all those children, and he needed help. So, he taught her the fine art of being a pastry chef and a wonderful one she was! She did all of the gourmet salad and dessert preparations in this European Plan hotel. (Three meals a day served to all the guests, included in their rates.) Holl's Inn is still operated this way. Of course, in those days, I think we opened in early June, and closed in late September. Guests came with their entire families, many by train to Thendara, where our Holl's Inn station wagon met them. Many stayed for several weeks, or even a month or more to escape the city heat.

What did Oscar, Hans, and Anna do the other eight months of the year? Much

Bobby and Helen
in their "uniforms"

needed maintenance, and lots of snow shoveling. Hans was the carpenter and Oscar, the electrician, Anna, the housekeeper and mother. It was April 1940, that I was born, soon to be followed by my brother Robert John (Bobby) in June of 1941. So, in the winter months, Mother cooked and made almost all of my clothes and Bobby's. My dresses were made from those colorful, flowered, chicken feed bags. And she always made a dress to match for my doll, Hilda. She also made uniforms for me and Bobby, copying the staff's uniforms. My slacks, or "pants," as she called them, and Bobby's were made from Uncle Oscar's fine cast-off trousers. Being a bachelor until he was 51, traveling some in winters, and being the handsome host at the Inn, necessitated fine attire. Oscar was drafted into the army during World War II, opposing his native Germany.

My parents sold their half of Holl's Inn to Oscar and his bride, Rosemary, in 1951. We then purchased Dibbles Inn in Vernon, N.Y. and ran it from then until 1956. The pressures of owning an excellent restaurant, along side the new race track, proved overwhelming for both Anna and Hans. Also, Hans was again longing for the Adirondacks, and what he thought would be a less stressful life. So, in February of 1956, he bought the Albedor on Fourth Lake. My brother and I were back with our classmates from Inlet, who were now in the upper grades in Old Forge. Mother and Daddy again ran a wonderfully successful business, and continued there until May of 1966, when my father passed away. Finally, he could rest.

Mother never went back into the Albedor after his death. They had bought a home on First Lake some years before as an investment. It was here that Mother lived until August 1, 1994, when a fall forced her into a retirement home for seventeen months. She passed away with my daughter, Jill, by her side, on January 30, 1996. Hans, Anna, and Bobby are all buried in Riverview Cemetery in Old Forge. Oscar died on April 4, 1993.

* * *

GRAND VIEW HOTEL, FOURTH LAKE, ADIRONDACKS.   Pub. by H. D. Ross, Inlet, E. Utica, N. Y.

Grand View Hotel

Farther down the South Shore of Fourth Lake was the Grand View Hotel, built in 1916 and run by J.J. Rarick. It housed a popular grocery store and was to become the site for children's camps.

Not all of the old hotels were on Fourth Lake. Located farther up the chain of lakes was the Seventh Lake House. Lynda Smith Kellogg has written a detailed history of this popular Adirondack Hotel:

> The original Seventh Lake House was built in the early 1900s by Duanne Norton. Mr. Norton came to Hamilton County from Lewis County where he owned and operated a sawmill. With lumber from his mill, he built the Seventh Lake House on the north shore of Seventh Lake, across the lake from the present day restaurant with the same name. According to an article written by M.P. Salvatore for the *Adirondak Express*, Mr. Norton hoped to attract people who wanted to get deeper into the woods than Old Forge or Eagle Bay. He was unsuccessful in his operation of the hotel due to its inaccessibility.
>
> Reaching the Seventh Lake House was a long and arduous trip. Travelers would first have to reach the city of

Seventh Lake House

Utica. From Utica, they would take a train approximately 55 miles to the station in Thendara. In Thendara they would either take another train or carriage the two miles to the lakefront in Old Forge and then a steamboat up the lakes or board a train for Eagle Bay station. At the station in Eagle Bay it was another 32 miles by carriage to the Seventh Lake House. The road from Eagle Bay to Inlet was very rough and heavily rutted. It is said that the trip from Utica to Inlet, approximately 70 miles, would sometimes take five hours.

Upon the death of Mr. Norton, the hotel was sold to Mr. Frank Williams, who in turn sold it to his brother, Charles Williams of Big Moose Lake. According to the article by Mr. Salvatore, Charles Williams made extensive repairs to the buildings and grounds, including the addition of an oval dining room. Frank Breen, the brother-in-law of Mr. Williams' son Fred, and his wife were hired to manage the hotel. The hotel began to prosper.

After the death of Charles Williams, the hotel passed to his son Fred. It was then sold to Fred's youngest daughter Elisabeth (Nibs) and her husband John Perry (Pitt) Smith.

The Smiths moved to Inlet from Syracuse in the mid 1940's with their two young daughters Lynda and Janice (Pookie) and would operate the hotel for the next ten years.

The Smiths made many improvements and repairs, as the hotel had sat idle for a few years. Private bathrooms and new kitchen facilities were added, along with a lot of new paint. The Smiths also added two more children to their family, another daughter Martha, and a son Fred.

During this time the hotel became a very popular vacation resort, attracting visitors from as far away as South America. Many traveled from the New York City area in the summer to escape the city heat. One family from Long Island came for a two week stay that lasted the whole summer due to the polio outbreak. The father would travel back down state every other week for work, leaving his family in Inlet. Syndicated cartoonist, Fred Neher, spent many summers at the Seventh Lake House. He would occasionally use the hotel and hosts in his cartoons.

One of the highlights of the summers were the weekly "cookouts" at the end of Seventh Lake. Pitt would hire Norton

Directions to Seventh Lake House

"Buster" Bird's boat, the Osprey, and load all the guests for a cookout consisting of steak, fried potatoes, corn on the cob, and dessert. This was usually cooked up by Pitt and his good friend and Adirondack guide, Don "Red" Perkins.

Winters at Seventh Lake were spent filling icehouses and woodsheds for the coming summer season. Ice was brought in from Big Moose and was important for the refrigeration of the food for the hotel. Wood fires were used for heat and the hot water for all six cottages and the hotel. As was the way of the time, the Seventh Lake House served three meals per day: breakfast, dinner, and supper, everything was fresh and homemade. The hotel had its own garden, but because the growing season is so short in the Adirondacks, it is doubtful that many of the vegetables on the tables were from this garden. Dinner was the largest meal and consisted of homemade soups, roasted pork, beef or poultry, potatoes, fresh vegetables, and delicious desserts. There were fresh pies, cakes, cookies, and even homemade ice cream made daily. Supper was a lighter meal of steak or chops, potatoes, vegetables, and more desserts. The Seventh Lake House operated until the summer of 1954, when the hotel was sold and later sub-divided and auctioned off. Today, the only original structures are some of the cottages, along with the laundry building and part of the woodshed which had the men's quarters in the second story.

Not to be forgotten is Limekiln Lake, rather secluded from the village of Inlet, but still a part of it. Here on these isolated shores was yet another hotel, Delmarsh Inn, opened around 1915 and operated by Archie Delmarsh's brother Eri. The Inn's brochure states that, "There are no clearings and all is as Mother Nature made it. No attempt is made at formality at Delmarsh Inn. Everything is homelike and comfortable," and goes on to say that, "Leaving New York City after breakfast, the traveler reaches the Inn in time for supper."

Also opened on Limekiln Lake at about the same time was the Lime Kiln Lake Hotel operated by Wallace Darling.

Delmarsh Inn

Lime Kiln Lake Hotel Dining Room

Lime Kiln Lake Hotel

-2-

Steamboats

ransportation to these hotels was rarely a simple proposi-
tion, in spite of the Rocky Point brochure that states "it is
easy of access by fine state highway, by steamer through the lakes,
or by train to the Eagle Bay station" and Inlet Inn's equal reassurance that it was:

> ...conveniently reached by the N.Y.C.R.R. via Utica,
> N.Y. and Clearwater on the Adirondack division, transfer
> at Clearwater to Raquette Lake R.R. to Eagle Bay Station
> thence by steamer one and one-quarter miles to hotel or
> you can change cars at Fulton Chain Station to Old Forge,
> thence by an interesting trip (12 miles) by steamer
> through the chain of lakes to hotel.

I would have thought the trip rather daunting.
The stately steamers plying the waters were certainly a prominent sight on the lakes, transporting tourists to these remote resorts
for recreation and sightseeing. The first known steamboat to travel
the area was the Hunter, in 1883, but perhaps one of the most well
known of these was the Clearwater. Built in 1900 and called the
Pride of Steamers, it could carry 300 people. In 1926, due perhaps
to the completion of the road from Old Forge to Eagle Bay, the
Clearwater stopped regular trips. Beached in First Lake, it burned
in 1938, like so many relics of this historic era.

The Clearwater

A postcard from the times shows the Clearwater loading, with the side tugboat also filled to overflowing. Apparently these side boats were also used for stability, as the steamers could be top-heavy at times.

The Nehasane

Other steamboats of the time had unusual and picturesque names, including the You-Go-I-Go, the Uncas, the Tuscarora, the Irocosia, the Mohegan, and the Nehasane.

Another of the steamboats was affectionately referred to as the "Pickle Boat" (although the name on its bow is the Mohawk) because of the large barrel of pickles it carried on the rear deck. It had 300 feet of shelf space and ran for thirty-four years, carrying needed supplies to campers and hotels when land transportation was still somewhat of a problem. When its days of usefulness on the water were over, the Pickle Boat entertained children at the Enchanted Forest in Old Forge as the adventurous Pirate Ship.

The other utilitarian boat was the mail boat, begun in the 1890s, supposedly at the request of President Benjamin Harrison, who had a camp on the lake. Still in service today, it has faithfully delivered to private docks up and down the lakes for more than 100 years. The job is somewhat precarious as the boat does not stop, but a deliv-

The "Pickle Boat"

erer must lean out to hand the mailbag to someone on the dock, ready to receive it, and in turn accept a mailbag back with his other hand. A rope holds him in the boat while his hands are busy. One fatal accident happened during the early time of the mail boat. The holding rope broke while the clerk was handing out the mail. He fell, hitting his head against the side of the dock, and was drowned.

Another spectacular event occurred when the mail boat sank and a crane from the deck of the Clearwater was employed to haul it back up and return it to operation.

The mail boat eventually was responsible for the dredging of the channel to make it deep enough for bigger boats to access a waterway to the town of Inlet. In 1948, when the hotel where the mail boat was accustomed to dock at the head of the lake refused further docking privileges, the town hired a contractor to make the channel

The mail boat   *The Clearwater and the mail boat*

deep enough for the mail boat to travel as far as the Post Office.

The other recorded disaster among all this boat traffic in the early days involved a small boat called the Caprice, which was carrying a load of lumber when it sank just off Cedar Island. Arch and Eri Delmarsh, who were building an icehouse on the island, heard the shouts and rowed out to rescue the occupants. One person was trapped in a cabin and died.

Although the name of the boat in the picture on the next page is the Marjorie, the legend on the back states that it was formerly the Caprice, and that it sank on November 22, 1902, and was raised on August 6, 1904. In the picture are William Bowman on the bow and his sister, Harriet Bowman in the pilothouse door; the other passengers are unidentified.

However, both the name of the boat, and the recovery of the body are uncertain. A newspaper account from that time describes the accident:

> The sad fatality of Saturday afternoon, when the steamer Marjorie, sank in Fourth Lake, at a point near Cedar Island, causing the death by drowning of Burt P. Murdock, a popular guide of this place, has left the locality under a pall of sorrow. A severe storm and too great a cargo brought about the catastrophe. There were four passengers on the steamer in addition to the guide at the time, but they escaped with their lives. The boat has been located in 622 feet of water, but the victim's body has not as yet been recovered. Mr. Murdock was in his 34th year and was unmarried.

Two years later, the following article appeared in a paper:

The little steamer, Marjorie, which was sunk near Cedar Isle, Fourth Lake, about two years ago, has been located. Diver Rulison, who has been at work two days, found the boat slightly turned on its left side, but not sufficient to be relieved of its cargo, and under 73 feet of water. The body of Burt Murdock, a boat hand, who went down with the steamer, was found in the stern end, apparently in a perfect state of preservation.

Burt Murdock

The copy of the article had been amended, with the information about Murdock crossed out by hand and annotated to say "body never found, Don, A.C.M."

The Marjorie

-3-

Children's Camps

As more and more of the wealthy looked to the Adirondacks for rest and recreation, so too did their children, and children's camps began to become increasingly popular. One of these, Camp Lo Na Wo, was opened in 1925 on the site of the former Grand View Hotel. Located on the South Shore of Fourth Lake, about a mile from Inlet, this was a camp for one hundred and twenty-five girls. Apparently the Depression caused its demise.

A rather interesting sidelight is that the boys' camp managed by the same directors was called Camp Swastika. The emblem was supposedly a good luck symbol used by the Indians and ran the opposite way from the Nazi logo. I remember one of these symbols painted on a large leather background and hanging in our family's camp when I was a child.

Camp Lo Na Wo was briefly held by Dr. Longstaff under the name Camp Eagle Cove, but this effort also failed. By 1937, Camp Eagle Cove was operating again under the direction of Ellen Hayes and Helmy Smirnova, still catering exclusively to girls. A brochure published at the time says that the facility lies in a:

> ...sheltered cove which allows instruction in canoeing and swimming to progress with safety and comfort.

Camp Lo Na Wo (later Camp Eagle Cove)

It further explains that:

> The central campus around which the bungalows are
> grouped is a large quadrangle of level ground that con-
> tains a hockey field, hand-ball, and volley ball courts, an
> archery range, and a badminton court.

The brochure also advertises "riding horses of a caliber greatly
higher than usually found in camp." There were fifteen bungalows
to house older campers, while the younger ones stayed in a "Junior
House" with two bathrooms and eight bedrooms. There were many
other buildings, including the impressive structure in the preceding
picture which hung over the water's edge and housed the large dining room with a pavilion above for recreation and dancing.

The fee, in 1937, for attending from July 1 until August 26, was
two hundred and seventy-five dollars. The brochure notes that
Camp Cedar Isles for boys is but a mile away and offers a discount
if both camps are attended by siblings.

Later, Camp Eagle Cove became a Jewish camp that enrolled

Central campus of Camp Eagle Cove

Riding horses at Camp Eagle Cove

Swim time at Camp Eagle Cove

Story time in the recreation building at Camp Eagle Cove

boys for one of the summer months and girls for the other.

A history of the camp would not be complete without mention of Joseph (Bellow) Snyder, a basketball pro from Rochester, New York, who directed the camp with great dedication for many years. Under Bellow's supervision, the camp custom at the end of the summer was to provide a one- or two-week basketball clinic, at which name players such as "Dolph" Shayes from the Syracuse Warriors would coach young hopefuls in the art of basketball. So great was Bellow's interest in the camp that when he finally retired, it was with the condition that Eagle Cove continue as a children's camp throughout his lifetime, and this condition was respected.

Upon his death, the property was purchased by Lynn University in the hope of establishing a northern campus in connection with the Florida-based Boca Raton college. One of the first things the university did after acquiring the prop-

Cedar Isles stone recreation hall

erty was to blast the large rock at the entrance, destroying the giant eagle painted thereon which had greeted all visitors to the site for so many years. The college was not successful at this location, and the shore that was once filled with sound and activity is now silent.

Another girls' camp was established at Cedar Island in 1915, when Mr. Berg bought the long-time hotel complex from E. S. Demarsh following a fire. He repaired the building and added several sleeping cabins, but his tenure as camp owner ended in 1932, when a second fire resulted in the property's foreclosure.

The next owner was Dr. Longstaff, who bought the property in 1933 to open a boys' camp. Fire struck the unfortunate island yet again in August of that year, destroying many of the buildings, but the campers were able to complete the season by eating their meals at the nearby Mohawk Hotel. Longstaff rebuilt and continued to operate the camp until 1950.

Cedar Isles

Swimming instruction at Cedar Isles

After Dr. Longstaff closed his camp, the island was abandoned, and it became a favorite place for the youth on the surrounding shores to explore and camp. All that remained intact of the original buildings were the stone recreation hall and the shell of the large boathouse which stood vigil on the eastern end of the island, over-looking the ruins. Much to the disappointment of its young explorers, the island was sold around 1960. The current owner restored some of the buildings and opened a summer ballet program. The stone house where adventurous boys loved to camp is now used as a practice room.

Camp Assisium

Another children's camp in those early years was Camp Assisium, located at the head of Fourth Lake just over the hill from town, at the site now occupied by Stiefvater's. It was originally founded as a rest camp for the Franciscan sisters from St. Elizabeth's Hospital in Utica. One of those nuns, Sister Della Rosa, had administered for a long time to lumberjacks in the area, visiting them in remote clearings and caring for them when mishaps took them to St. Elizabeth's. When she asked for their support of this project, the lumberjacks gave it willingly.

In 1926, the property was acquired by Rev. Joseph May, director for youth at Catholic Charities in Utica. At first, the camp was used exclusively by boys, accommodating 120 at a time. Eventually girls were also admitted. Reverend May was honored in 1952 for founding the camp and serving as its executive officer for twenty-five years.

-4-

Buildings and Businesses

As one rises over the crest of the hill on the way into town, the sight of the village of Inlet nestled in the valley below is always a welcome one. It must have been even more so to the travelers of an earlier time when every trip was so much more arduous.

The picture at the top of the next page shows what those early travelers would have seen. On the right is the site of the three old Parquet buildings. The original owner, Fred Parquet, was a merchant who ran a small rooming house on the side. The two buildings at the far right will eventually be used as post office buildings. The larger building will become a restaurant with the very popular Rathskellar in the basement. Fire swept through the restaurant in the early morning hours of July 6, 1962, destroying it completely and threatening the entire business section. The smaller building on the right was spared and is still used as a rooming house.

Across the road to the left is the Inlet Supply Company, built by Herman Williston in 1938. This continues as a successful business place through today, though it has known many owners over the years. Floyd Puffer was one, as were co-owners Len Harwood and Lansing Tiffany. Tiffany was also County Judge, Surrogate, and Children's Court Judge, and the surrogate's safes were lined up in his store along with the gas stoves and other appliances. Upstairs was the court room, with a nice view of Fourth Lake. At the time,

Inlet Supply Co, General Store, Church, and Post Office

The Village of Inlet

An early photo of the Parquet

A photo of the later Parquet before it was destroyed by fire

Inlet Supply Company

LANSING TIFFANY, who runs the Inlet hardware store, is county
judge, surrogate, and children's court judge for Hamilton County,
the "Northwest Territory" of New York State.

Lansing Tiffany

the judge did not need to be a lawyer. Harwood, the other owner, was Town Supervisor at this time, so the store was a convenient place to catch up on town business while buying a saw.

At one time, Margaret Graves had a small but flourishing gift shop on the right side of the same building.

The other buildings shown in the old photograph of the town are the Church of the Lakes with the manse beside it and a garage behind the manse. Dedicated on September 18, 1901, the chapel became one of the newest structures in the newly formed town. The church occupies the same lot to this day, although the building was moved back from the road and a side room was added.

As Howard Weiman narrated in his history of the church:

William D. And Gertrude Moshier gave property in the Town of Morehouse to the Presbytery in 1900 to build a church with the stipulation that at least ten services would be held each year. A year later part of the Town of Morehouse was split off and the Town of Inlet was created. The Board of National Missions gave a $500.00 grant mortgage bond to the Utica Presbytery to aid in construction of a church in 1901. The Church

Bell at Church of the Lakes

of the Lakes began as a mission chapel of Niccoll's Church of Old Forge and was dedicated in September of 1901. Reverend Howard Wallace, who was the area missionary, was the first minister of this chapel. The church was the first building on the north side of the road, and was moved back from the road to permit the construction of Route 28 around 1914. A basement and social room were added to the church at this time. In December 1920, the congregation was organized as Church of the Lakes, enrolled with the Presbytery of Utica in February 1921, and became incorporated in 1926. The church was electrified in 1925. The highway was finally completed in 1928 after long delays when the first contractor went bankrupt.

Weiman goes on to say that Albert A.C. and Caroline L. Boshart gave property to the Presbytery in 1913 and 1918 for a manse. O.M. Edwards then gave a substantial amount of money so a proper plan could be drawn, and the manse was finished in 1914. The icehouse and garage which were soon added behind the buildings can be seen in the picture of the old town (top of page 42). Reverend David Davies was the first resident minister to occupy the manse.

Pictured: Bob Bird, Jack Hall, Stu Nelson, Betty Nelson, Freida Nelson, Olive Clark, Toni Baerman, Dick Baerman, Ruth Nelson, Henry Smith, Bill and Olive Netherton, with Una Lewis at the organ; others are unidentified.

A list of early ministers includes:

Reverend R. Howard Wallace: 1901–1904
Reverend George VanDyke: 1904–1905
Reverand Richard Hughes: 1905
Reverend Clarence Gee: 1912
Reverend David Davies: 1914
Reverend Albert McClements: 1921–1922
Reverend Almond C. Dodge: 1923–1924
Reverend Herbert N. Baird: 1925–1928
Reverend George R.J. Combs: 1929–1933
Reverend Charles McClure: 1934–1936
Reverend Frank Reed: 1937–1938
Reverend R.H. Roche: 1939–1942

The Reverend Herbert Baird wrote a history of the church in which were included some interesting personal recollections. He recounts the advice he received from a previous minister, Reverend Davies: "Expect to have a number of ministers in the summer congregations. They would come to worship if they were not called out of the pews into the pulpit." At one service he counted eleven of them, but he found them to be the least critical members of the congregation.

He continues explaining that when the need for small chairs for the newly established kindergarten became known, a local Ku Klux Klan group contributed the money to purchase little red chairs. He adds that when he was invited to attend one of the Klan's meetings, he found it much like a church prayer service.

His description of life in the winter seems worth repeating:

Winter brought a change of life in the community. Roads were plowed with a wooden woods plow, drawn by a team and later by a Linn tractor. The plow left a road wide enough for one car, with a ridge in the center. When another car was met, both drivers shared in the shoveling of a turn-out, unless a convenient driveway, or the activity of earlier travelers, provided a place to pass. After a time, the ridge in the center froze solid, and required chopping to permit the cars to pull out of the ruts; or, forehanded

Chapel of the Lakes, Inlet, Adirondacks.

Original Church of the Lakes

drivers might carry a few pieces of firewood to place in the ruts to aid in getting out. The South Shore Road was not plowed from the Inlet town line to the Adirondack League Club and one could not drive beyond McKeever, or north of Raquette Lake until the winter road was plowed across the lake. The Raquette Lake Railroad provided rail connections with the Adirondack Division of the New York Central at Carter, but in the winter only [on] Monday, Wednesday, and Saturday. On the off days, it was necessary to drive to Thendara to get outside. I remember going to Presbytery in April by train, because the road through Woodgate was still deep in snow.

He added:

One of the fringe benefits of the Inlet pastor was the icehouse, which the men of the church filled each year. Usually this was done before the ice on the lake was no more than a foot thick, but one year the harvest was delayed. Then one block was cut—a perfect three foot cube.

Alladin mantle lamps provided the best available illumination. Telephone service for most residents was limited to a purely local system, with the instrument, hand cranked, provided by the owner. There was no exchange, but each home had its own ring code, that was heard on every other phone. There was an advantage, in that one could answer their phone at any other phone upon hearing their number. Of course, one did not discuss any very personal matters with that kind of phone system.

By 1927, a chapel had been opened in Raquette Lake, and Reverend Baird was to preach there as well as at Inlet. He traveled the Uncas Road, which was not always in the best condition due to mud or snow.

There were times in the winter when the road was impassible due to snow, and the railroad track was better, if a bumpier way. On occasion, Mr. Wilbur, the Inlet school principal, accompanied me with the thought that two would be better than one if there were problems. One spring night, returning from an evening service at Raquette, the car dropped into a deep hole so that the rear housing rested on the ground and the wheels spun uselessly in the mud puddles on both sides. I walked back to the Bird home at Raquette, and spent the rest of the night on their couch. The next morning the section gang was going my way. I went with them, the car being at a place where the track and road ran side by side. They cut poles in the woods to raise the car, and filled the hole with old railroad ties. When I stopped at the Inlet post office, the post mistress remarked that I must have been in the mud somewhere.

Many people traveling in those days on these precarious roads must have had similar experiences.

It would be negligent to leave this history of the Church of the Lakes without commenting on the rift that resulted in the establishment of a second church. This disagreement occurred around 1953. At that time, a new organ was acquired and unfortunately was viewed by some members as such a valuable possession that no one save the current organist could touch it. A student from Eastman School of Music in Rochester was denied access to the organ, but more importantly, when the town wanted to use it for a civic production, a faction of the church refused. Since there was a sizable number that thought it should be shared, a dispute ensued that was so unreconcilable that many members departed from the church and formed what is now known as the Community Church.

Not visible in the early pictures was the building on the corner of the South Shore road where Screamen Eagle Pizza now stands. This was originally a grocery store opened by Walter Rosa, at least by 1923.

The town was growing, and with growth came new businesses. There were an increasing number of privately owned automobiles that required servicing, a need that was filled when Army's Garage and Service Station was built and operated by W. Lewis Armstrong in 1925. This establishment stood on the opposite corner of the South Shore Road from Rosa's grocery store. Although it may have had other owners, my memory of it was when Bob and Ted Harwood ran it for many years.

Many of the young local boys liked to hang out at the garage, including the Haynes and Rudd boys. Ted Harwood recalls that one of the Rudds didn't like noise and would always ask, "Are you

Inlet Garage

going to be making noise?" before he would enter.

In 1930, Mary and Dan Decker opened a gift shop on the Navigation Dock, but soon moved their business to the present location on the right side of the road entering Inlet from the South. It looks today much as it did then, though it has seen many owners.

When Harry Hall came to the Adirondacks in 1919, he was employed as a grocery clerk for Walt Rosa. In 1921, Hall formed a partner-ship with Bowen, purchasing a lot from the Boshart property next to Mary's Gift Shop. Their store opened in 1922. When the partnership was dissolved in 1923, the business became known as Hall's Store and added a door-to-door milk delivery business, covering the territory from Remsen

Mary's Gift Shop

to Blue Mountain Lake. In the early years, trucks were used for delivery in the summer, and horse-drawn sleighs made deliveries in the winter. At the height of the season, Hall employed seven trucks. The milk was carried in large cans and dispensed by dipper-full into the customer's own container. During the 1930s Hall also operated a supply boat on Sixth and Seventh Lakes, providing goods to campers in the summertime. Upon his death, his son Jack took over the store. This building has housed many businesses, but at present stands empty with a "For Sale" sign in the window.

Wilkins' fascinating Indian Craft Shop was perched on the left side of the crest of the hill heading north into Inlet. The shop was made all the more interesting because of the various levels caused by its hillside location. I was happy to finally find someone who remembers, as I do, that the shop started as a tent on the rise across from the present Post Office, where the Inlet Gift Center is located today.

In the Syracuse Herald-American of August 19, 1979, an article by Marion Tubbs described the tent where:

Hall's Store

Interior view of Hall's Store

Mrs. Wilkins sold straw and reed baskets and beautiful novelties such as pine cone hanging baskets, woven moccasins and balsam pillows. At the rear of the tent, you could watch the weaver, an elderly Indian, at work. It was a trick to reach the wooden platform at the entrance with clean shoes, since the path from the road was soft pasture land.

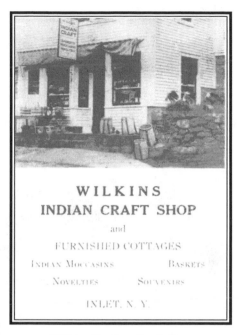

Wilkins' Indian Craft Shop

The Wilkins' shop at the entrance to town opened in 1939; the building still stands at the crest of the hill but is now a private residence.

About this time Dewey Rudd bought the building across from the Church of the Lakes and converted it to a Red and White grocery store. It stayed in the Rudd family for many years.

Another grocery store was in existence at least by 1925, with John Simon as proprietor. It stood where Ace Hardware is now located. I remember it because my mother, who didn't drive in those days, took us there shopping. On one occasion, when we left with arms burdened with groceries, someone offered to drive us

The Red & White grocery store

John Simon Groceries

Trottier's Restaurant

home. The car was small, so my sister and I were relegated to the rumble seat—my one and only ride in one, but still vivid in my memory. This may have been when someone other than John Simon owned the store.

Beside this store was the restaurant of Fred Trottier, opened by 1925. Trottier was instrumental in forming the fire company, and it was he who spread the word about the Gaity Theater fire, as told later on in this book.

Other stores were gradually added. The Jack and Jill Gift Shop opened under the ownership of the benevolent George and Mildred Blakeman. Here, a child could sit under the overhanging roof in the rocking chair conveniently provided, and read comic books to his heart's content, without ever having to buy one.

Vonglis's Sweet Shop was between the Jack and Jill and the Inlet Supply, but we are verging on a newer era.

Let's follow the road up over the hill beyond the Red and White. On the left is St. Anthony's Church. At the time the ministry started in 1911, the spiritual concerns of the people of Inlet were being met by the resident pastor of Old Forge. By 1914, the town had grown and was large enough to warrant a church of its own. Jennie C. Galvin donated the site, and the attractive frame building now known as St. Anthony's was completed in 1915. Franciscan Alphonse Vollmer supervised the construction and was in charge of the mission until 1919. He was succeeded by Franciscan Hillary Hemmer, OFM. This appointment changed the status of the church to a parish, with Father Hemmer becoming the first rector.

In 1922, Father Hemmer acquired more property, and the present rectory was completed in the spring of 1923. He retired in 1926 because of ill health and was succeeded on March 18 of that year by the Rev. Thomas Grassman, under whom St. Anthony's became a year-round church. The care of the Holy Rosary Mission at Big Moose was then transferred from Raquette Lake to Inlet. Father Grossman took up residence as permanent rector on March 18, 1926.

Through Father Thomas's direction, a community hall was built and dedicated on July 13, 1927. The church was badly damaged by fire on October 21, 1928, but was immediately rebuilt and enlarged. A new pipe organ was installed and the building rededicated on August 3, 1929.

On September 29, 1929, the church was officially incorporated under the guidance of the Most Reverend Bishop P.S. Garand,

Early St. Anthony's Church *St. Anthony's Church*

Reverend Thomas Grassman, Lansing K. Tiffany, and Bernard O'Hara.

On the shores of picturesque Fifth Lake stand the town's two school buildings. Although the sign in front of the Inlet Common School today proclaims to passers-by that the school was established in 1906, the land was deeded on January 4, 1901, to Charles O'Hara as trustee of School District 4 of the Town of Morehouse (by James and Jennie Galvin for $76.13), so it is probable that the "little" school opened before that. In fact, Carl Smith, the present custodian, says the words "ready for school 1903" are carved on a beam in the attic of the bigger building. If that building was in use by then, it would seem the smaller one had to have been in use perhaps as early as the fall of 1901. Mary Jane Delmarsh, daughter of the first Archie Delmarsh to run Rocky Point, believes her mother Laura Kirch Delmarsh was the first teacher at the school when she worked there before her marriage. And since the 1900 census lists Laura Kirch as "teacher," it seems evident that there was indeed a school at that time.

Other early teachers included Alice Burdick, Ann Burdick, Wilmer Hawthorne, Mrs. Raymond Norton, Mary Puffer Canfield, Bernard O'Hara, Alton O'Hara, John Rogers, George Blakeman Sr., Mildred Puffer, and Madeline Wood.

Whatever the opening date, the school has struggled and succeeded

*A picture from an old newspaper shows one of the early classes with their teachers.
Pictured are Linda Smith, Audrey Payne, Guy Delmarsh, Kit Delmarsh,
Ann Delmarsh, Harry Delmarsh, Kay Delmarsh, Archie Delmarsh,
Brenda Meneilly, Patty Tiffany, Jim Payne, Robert Bird, Don Bird, Joe Kopp,
Claire Puffer, Jackie Burth, Joyce Houck, Bob Merriman, Janet Scott,
Dick Clark, Kay Gribneau, John Kalil, Peter Kalil, Jack McNeil, Helen Holl,
Larry McNeil, and Joan Payne; the teachers are
Marge Cornbloom and Ruth Rarrick.*

*Another school picture taken in 1918, though not very clear, shows the following
people: Miss Osgood and Miss Falin, teachers; Rose Blakeman, Clifford Puffer,
Mildred Puffer, Winifred Van Arnam, Ritha Blakeman, Louise Porter, Ruth Blair,
Marjorie Wood, George Blakeman, Marion Puffer, Alice Ford, Ruth Kenwell, Iva
Lucas, Thelma Parquet, Phyllis Trottier, Grace Lucas, Gertrude Puffer, Charlie
Blair, Edith Gilgrist, Daphne Trottier, Ella Rogers, Beatrice Rogers, Arthur
Luca, Jr., Alton O'Hara, John Rogers, Orvis Porter, Graden Hildrith, Lewis
Puffer, James Menneilly, Jr., and Marshall Brown. One child is unidentified.*

in maintaining its unique, one-room school atmosphere in spite of drastic reductions in population and several attempts to close it.

Farther up the road on the rushing stream between Fifth and Sixth Lakes is the sawmill, built by the enterprising Fred Hess in 1892. The spot was ideal, as the surrounding forests seemed capable of yielding an unending supply of logs. Thus the logging industry in its various forms was one of the primary sources of income in the community. The mill ran on the abundant water power from the nearby stream, aided by the

Inlet school buildings

dam Hess built at the foot of Sixth Lake. An unfortunate by-product of the mill, the sawdust created during processing, was dumped into the stream, where it floated for a while, then rotted and sank. The site of the sawmill was approximately where the Easy Mart or Laundry Mart stands today.

Sometime in this period the Fifth Lake Inn was opened, nearly across from the sawmill. It was later owned by Bill Patrick, whose son, Bernard, worked for a long time in the Inlet Post Office.

By 1925, Elwood Searles, a former marine engineer, opened a garage across from the school. It was later expanded and owned by Joe Payne. The property has stayed in the Payne family ever since, though used for other purposes.

Hess's sawmill

Fifth Lake Inn

Elwood Searles' Garage

Payne's Garage

-5-

Recreation

Although people had to work almost constantly just to sustain life in those early years, they still found time for recreation, and perhaps enjoyed it more.

Hunting and fishing continued to be popular, and then as now, beginning in 1931, fish were released to supplement the natural ones. They were brought in pails by trucks in those early days, not by the helicopters that are used today. Rabbits were also released to be hunted (which seems to me to be a cruel thing to do).

While these activities perhaps contributed to a needed food supply, other activities that developed were just for fun.

Probably the most spectacular was the 660-foot toboggan run built in 1935 at a cost of $5,000. It hurled courageous souls from high above the highway at the site of the present boat launch, out onto frozen Fourth Lake, and ended in a slide across the ice nearly to Cedar Island. In 1942, when the run was getting too little use to warrant its upkeep, it was removed.

When The Old Forge Electric Company and Archie Delmarsh gave land to the town for a skating rink in 1935, ice hockey became a major winter sport, attracting players from as far as Canada and an audience from miles around. A newspaper article from January 11 states:

Upwards of 1,000 persons flocked to this village over the weekend for the official open-ing of the sports program which is being sponsored here this season.

The tobaggan slide was dedicated Saturday by Miss Ella Rogers, and proved a highly popular pastime with coasters using the $5,000 slide until after midnight Saturday, and in a continuous stream today.

Two hockey games featured the programs. Saturday, Inlet bowed to the Speculator team, 1-0. Today, the Durhams and Black and Inlet sextets battled through 60 minutes of play and an overtime period, but neither was able to score.

Fish being released

Rabbits being released

The toboggan run

On January 26, the enthusiasm continues in another newspaper account which states:

> Winter sports are now at their peak in Inlet, the White Playground of the Central Adirondacks, with the recent heavy fall of snow contributing to the delights and thrills of sport lovers.
>
> Preeminent among the attractions at Inlet is the mammoth double track toboggan slide which has just recently been completed. Later on, it is expected that the slide will be enlarged, making it to continue up the mountain side.
>
> Other popular sports at Inlet include skating on Fourth Lake, skiing down the mountain slopes, skijoring, and winter baseball.
>
> Ice hockey with its speed and intense fascination has claimed Inlet guests and residents of the Central Adirondacks. Inlet is being represented by a team made up of the best available players of the north country and Canada. The Inlet sextet has given a very creditable account of itself already this season, losing only one game which was to the fast Speculator team, early in the winter.

View from the top of the toboggan run

The article continues by saying that:

Several of the popular hotels at Inlet have been fitted with heating plants and equipped with every comfort for the winter guest. The roads to Inlet will be kept open all winter in spite of the typical Adirondack snows. To meet this contingency, special motor plows have been purchased and these will not only keep the roads open, but plow them wide enough so that guests wishing to drive to Inlet will be able to do so without inconvenience.

There were rinks in at least two locations in Inlet. One was across from Stiefvater's, where the Black Bear Trading Post now stands; the other was in Arrowhead Park

Various forms of racing on the ice have always been popular. Trucks and cars were frequently seen engaging in this sport. While an onlooker might feel a little trepidation at hearing ice cracking around him, he could be reassured by watching the heavy snow plows clearing a track.

Bottom Row (left to right): Desbriens, Pelletier, Archambault.
Top Row (left to right): Fancher, Lafortune, Brunelle,
Gagnon (captain), Violette, Cloutier

Bottom Row (left to right): Ernie Satamore, Art Patrick, Don Delmarsh,
Bus Bird, Greg Delmarsh, George Blakeman
Top Row (left to right): Alec Oby, unknown, Jeff Lewis, Bob Wilkins,
Elwood Searles, Charles Cole, Lansing Tiffany

Arrowhead Park hockey rink

Car race on Fourth Lake

The snowmobile which was owned by the Church of the Lakes in Inlet. The vehicle was made by converting a Model T Ford and was used by the pastor to travel from church to church.

Skis, sleds, and once in a while, iceboats, also enjoyed racing on the frozen lakes. Snowmobiles, though occasionally used in desperate circumstances for transportation, were not at this time used for recreation, nor did they much resemble the vehicles used today.

Skiing was also becoming a greater attraction, though without the fancy boots and trappings used by today's skiers. This advertising brochure brought such spectacular results that the paper on Monday, January 20, 1936, reported:

"Trail!" This—the skier's equivalent of "Fore"—echoed on Adirondack mountain sides all day Sunday as the New York Central's somewhat experimental "snow train" tumbled 1,013 winter sports enthusiasts into the Old Forge area. They responded in such numbers that the train ran in two sections, one carrying 413 passengers from Utica, and another 600 from Syracuse. Successful in every way, the "snow train" gave every evidence of developing into an almost weekly mid-winter institution.

Advertisement for the "snow train"

The dance pavilion at Fern Park

Summer, of course, brought different types of recreation. In 1927, a baseball field was established at Fern Park under the directorship of Vernon Snyder and Floyd Puffer of Inlet and Robert Croadsdell of Eagle Bay, and a stadium was erected to accommodate enthusiastic supporters. Pictures from that time show that fans filled the stadium to overflowing.

The dance pavilion also located in Fern Park was the scene of many dances, both square and round.

For a time, horse shows were popular, attracting both riders and fans. In 1933 Harold Callahan won a trophy for "saddle horse championship" on his horse, Venice.

For evening entertainment, the Gaity Theater was opened in 1929 for movies and dances. It would be one-of-a-kind because, in 1942, heavy snow caused the building to collapse. Since World War II made rebuilding supplies unavailable, a Quanset hut was erected to house the theater. Though somewhat noisy,

Maurice and Mandel Schulman
in Quonset theatre with workers

The grandstand at Fern Park

*An early baseball team, including Joe Dunay (squatting center),
and Walter Moran (striped shirt)*

Inlet Golf Club

it served a useful purpose for many years. A rather unique feature at that time were the matinees that were offered on rainy days.

Sometime around 1926, an uncontrolled brush fire along the Limekiln Lake Road burned a large section of land before it was brought under control. Mindful of the need to attract ever greater numbers of tourists to the area, a group of Inlet businessmen decided to use the conveniently cleared land for a golf course. On July 27, 1926, the Inlet Golf Club was incorporated. Directors for the first year were Charles O'Hara, Archie Delmarsh, Frank Tiffany, W. Lewis Armstrong, Harry Hall, Floyd Puffer, and Frank Breen, all from Inlet, Dennis Dillon from Raquette Lake, and Roy Higby of Big Moose. They helped raise twenty-five thousand dollars by the time work was begun on the course. Larry McNeil was appointed the first professional, followed by Bert Young and Bud Hall. Another summer attraction had been added to call tourists to Inlet.

Golfers at the Inlet Golf Club (courtesy of the Town of Webb Historical Association)

Then as now, however, perhaps the most attractive aspect of Inlet was its striking beauty and the enormous number of recreational possibilities the community offered apart from organized activities. There were mountains to climb, hiking trails through the woods, an abundance of wild birds and animals, clear lakes for boating and swimming, ponds and sparkling streams reflecting sunlight or moonbeams, dazzling snow in winter, breathtaking colors in fall, and clear air to breathe all year round. All called to city dwellers to come and enjoy.

View from Rocky Mountain (originally called Nipple Top Mountain)

Scenic view of Fourth Lake

-6-

Public Services

*I*nlet seems to have started mail service on May 3, 1898. At that time, mail traveled by pack basket over a dirt path that wound its way along the northern shores of the Fulton Chain of Lakes. Charles O'Hara, the first town clerk, was also the first postmaster, and George Delmarsh was the second. They operated from a small wooden structure on the Wood Hotel lot. This building was eventually moved to the Old Barn property, long after it was no longer used as a post office.

When Fred Parquet became the next postmaster, he moved the service to his property. It was located first in the very small building seen in the picture and then in the larger one beside it. There appears to be a post office sign on the small building.

Eventually, space was leased from the Inlet Fire Department when their new building was constructed, and the Post Office still operates from that convenient location in the center of town.

Another service that was immediately necessary, as evidenced by the number of fires, was a fire department. However, the establishment of this much needed service was fraught with conflict, as so many of the improvements to the town seemed to be. The following story by Lewis Armstrong describes the controversy.

The first Post Office

THE PRETTY LITTLE POST OFFIG AT THE INLET N.Y ON 4TH LAKE.

Another view of the first Post Office

The Parquet and the Post Office, 1913

Post Office in the larger Parquet building

The True Story About How
the Inlet Volunteer Fire Co. Was Started
—by W. Lewis Army Armstrong

Back in 1923, in June, when I came to Inlet to stay and run the garage, we stood around and watched people's homes burn to the ground with no help at all. I didn't think that was right. I thought we needed a fire department so I set out to get one. I talked it over with a few of the men and they wanted to see a fire department also. So the first thing I did was to put up notices all over town, we were going to hold a meeting upstairs in Trottier's place to talk it all over. That we did, and the night of the meeting I stood downstairs and someone asked Frank Tiffany if he was going to the meeting and he said yes but it "won't amount to much." That made me mad and I lived to see the day the Inlet Volunteer Hose Co. Inc. did amount to a lot in that town. Well that meeting was just a meeting and every one had a say in what we should do. So we made the notice then of the next meeting which was to organize and elect a president, vice president, secretary, chief, 1st assistant chief and a 2nd assistant chief.

Then we had the organization meeting and I was elected president, Doc. Jones, vice-president, Fred Trottier, 1st assistant, and Dominick Fredette, 2nd assistant. So we had the Inlet Fire Company started. But the next meeting broke it all up and there was never any more Inlet Fire Company. At the meeting we had to vote on two new members, Clarence Lee and Evi Van Armum. Well they both got seven no votes and it came from one side of the room where the Puffers, Doc Snyder, George Blakeman, and Herman Williston were sitting. Well I went home mad. What kind of a fire department was I president of when right at the start they would try to keep men out of the department. So I had a talk with some of my friends like Fred Trottier, Modest (Fredette), Fred Parquey [sic], Roy Rogers, Charlie O'Hara, Len Harwood, Harry Hall. They all felt we should not let a few men stop us from having a fire department. So we called a special meeting in my kitchen and only had those who were invited.

So at that meeting in my kitchen, a new fire company was started called The Inlet Volunteer Hose Company and much later we incorporated. We bought an old Ford from C. Ray Harvey in Boonville and put a Ford and pump I had hooked up on it, and that was our first fire truck. Then the firemen started talking about real fire apparatus and so we got Joe Sullivan, who was a friend of mine, up to talk with us about what we should get. He had an All-American LaFrance in Utica so it was only natural we turned to LaFrance and soon the salesman came up to talk to us. It was going to cost us over $10,000.00 and we had about $100.00 in the bank. So we all talked it over and decided to try and raise the money by asking everyone for a donation. We did just that, and even Sears Roebuck came through with $25.00 for apparatus. We got a letter from the Raquette Lake Supply. They would give us $500.00, and we got many other letters telling us how much people would give toward a piece of fire apparatus. The down payment was going to be $3,500.00 so when we got way over the mark, I called a special meeting and we voted on whether we should order the apparatus or not. When we voted on anything like that, we had the secretary call the roll and each man got up and voted 'yes' or 'no'. Only two men voted 'no', Clarence Lee and Evi VanArmum. Clarence told about raising money for the church in Old Forge and how after people said they would give, then they dropped out and so they never raised the money. So at that meeting I asked Clarence if he had the cash would he vote for it, and he said 'yes'. Then we set out to get the money in cash, which we did in about two weeks. Then I called another special meeting and those two damn men still voted against buying the apparatus after they had said they would. So we bought the fire truck any way because I had the promise from Archie Delmarsh if we should lack a little money some year on our payment, he would help us out.

The apparatus came into Eagle Bay in a boxcar one Friday afternoon and Pop Mosher was there to unload it for us. It sure was a proud bunch of firemen who drove it over to Inlet. Guess who drove it! Well everybody turned out on Saturday to learn how to run it and it was very easy, and every fireman took his turn and did everything with it. So we put it in the tin shed by my house, and Len Harwood took Pop Mosher fishing Sunday up to Brown Track Pond near Raquette. About 10 A.M. that Sunday morning, Walt Rosa came running across the road to the garage that Mingo Lodge was on fire. So we went to work and I drove the fire truck. When we got there, no road at all to the lake and no man in his right mind would ever put an apparatus down that hill. But I wasn't in my right mind and I got it over the cesspool and down to where we could get water. The whole roof was on fire and a big line knocked that fire down fast. Then I took the big line into my connection for the booster line and just let the pump idle and we had water on the booster to clean up without getting too much water in the building. After we had been running that way about half an hour, Roy Rogers came up to me and said, "I never knew that chemical tank held so much water." He thought we were using a 40 gallon chemical tank all that while. After the fire was out, then came the job of getting the fire truck back on the road again. Well, it took about 50 men on ropes, and by bridging the cesspool and a lot of work, we got it out of there, and when Pop Mosher and Len got back and saw where I had put it, they knew I was crazy, but we put the fire out.

We had the fire truck about two weeks when we put it to the big test. Where the Legion has the ambulance now, (across from Mary's Gift Shop), was the Pavilion theatre. That was the night we could have lost the town without our fire truck. That caught on fire and I can see Fred Trottier running up the street yelling "Fire," so I got out the fire truck and went to work. We laid hose with it and put the truck back of Parquet's. Ben Sperry had one line in front of the building which he would put on Berkowitz's once in a while, and then on the Gaiety Theater, which is still standing today. Up on the roof of the Gaiety were Floyd Puffer and Harold Young and then their nozzle blew off and to get water on the fire they would squeeze the hose on the end. We had a garden hose on Ben with a blanket over him and it was still hot as hell.

An early picture of the Inlet Volunteer Fire Co.

But somehow we got the fire out and saved two buildings next door and all we had in the Gaiety was a couple of cracked windows. The building was scorched on the side but didn't burn. Within a couple of days, Chief Joe Sullivan came up from Utica and looked the job over and told me his men in Utica could not have saved the Gaiety. So we felt pretty good about our work.

Then in 1926, they elected me chief. Well, I didn't like the LaFrance, it was too big. We couldn't get it in many places we wanted to and so I talked the fire department into a small Chevrolet truck with a front mounted pump on it. Then we did go to work, for we could get that in most any place and we put out ten times as many fires with it as we did with the big truck. That's where the idea came for the "Little Mo," which is still the best fire truck for any fire department to have.

Well, that is the end of my story about the start of the Inlet Volunteer Hose Company, Inc. and how it started. Let someone else tell you about the building, but when we built it, Clarence Lee said none of us would ever live to see it paid for, and it was in five years.

The Great Water System Debate

Inlet never did manage to install a complete public water system, but the effort to do so has caused many a bitter battle over the years, the fracturing of long-standing friendships, and extensive and expensive lawsuits.

Wellington Kenwell

On July 25, 1910, Wellington Kenwell was given a franchise to construct a water line that serviced a limited area. Eventually C.F. Lee acquired the system, with Kenwell holding a $4,000 mortgage. In July 1930, when the town tried to promote a more extensive service, the owners of the private system opposed it, although the necessary fifty percent of the property owners approved the formation of a water district. After Robert Wheeler, the engineer in charge of the new system, was given permission on June 29, 1931, to cross three bridges with a water line, the opposition took drastic steps. When a special town meeting was called to conduct business about the new system, Supervisor Lee introduced Attorney Frank Bowman of Lowville, who announced that the meeting was illegal on the basis that it had not been properly advertised, even though it had been listed in the Adirondack Arrow for the three previous weeks. This meeting was therefore adjourned.

When thirty taxpayers petitioned for a another special meeting, one was held on July 2, 1931. It was decided to send Lee to the water commissioners, Col. Simmons, Frank Tiffany, and P. Elwood, to seek a solution. On July 11, 1931, bonds of $110,000 were authorized for the town water supply. Again Supervisor Lee balked.

On August 5, 1931, Attorney Alton O'Hara was authorized by the board to institute proceedings to compel the supervisor to "sign, issue, and deliver water bonds of $110,000." Determined to defeat the town, Kenwell had meanwhile started a suit charging that it would be illegal to use Bug Lake (the proposed water source), as it was state-owned.

On August 10, 1931, when the town board sought a compromise

with Kenwell, he threatened to shut off the water entirely, causing the Town Board of Health to enter the picture. Since users of the only existing water supply were unable to provide their own water system, the Board directed Lee to continue to supply water until another source could be found, thereby ensuring sanitary conditions. On August 14, the water commissioners offered to purchase Kenwell's system for $6,000. Instead, he brought a taxpayer's action against the officials of the town and the Inlet Water District Commission. The issue was tried in Supreme Court by Alton O'Hara, attorney for Kenwell, and by James Tormey, counsel for the Town of Inlet. The court decided in favor of Kenwell on the grounds that the bond sale was illegal. The town immediately applied for federal funds.

In large headlines, a newspaper article of the day proclaimed that, "Court Favors Owner of Old Water Supply" and went on to state that, "Wellington A. Kenwell, veteran guide and woodsman, has been informed the court of appeals has decided in his favor, bringing to an end the long-litigated Inlet water controversy that began when work was commenced on the new system." The town won in all courts until it reached the Court of Appeals, where the decision was in Kenwell's favor. The interpretation of that court was that the state has no right to allow the building of public reservoirs using state-owned water.

A year passed with no resolution, mounting bills, and growing enmity. Adding insult to injury, by September 1936, O'Hara and Tormey were suing the town for non-payment of their bills. The Board was unsure of its legal position and engaged yet another lawyer, attorney Kronmiller, to represent it.

Suits dragged on with partial payments made and percentages disputed. Finally, on September 19, 1938, the Town Board gave up. Seven years of fighting, with nothing to show for it but ill will and bills, was enough.

This was not the end of the battle, however. In 1945, the then health officer declared the water system unsafe. This stage of the ongoing issue continued for five years. In 1955, another phase of this struggle began as fruitlessly. No problem has caused the town so much in money, time, and shattered friendships. After all of this, Inlet still is without a public water system.

* * *

This was not the only subject of disharmony and contention in those formative years. As you will see in the next chapter, there was constant disagreement about the construction of roads.

* * *

Dr. R.G. Wallace from Eagle Bay seems to have been the first doctor to serve the town, but by 1904, he had moved from the area and a new health officer was being sought. Dr. Stewart Nelson from Old Forge was appointed to the position in 1908 and served until 1913, when Dr. Robert Lindsey replaced him. In 1917, Dr. J. S. Parker was employed as town physician, and he stayed until early 1920, followed by Dr. V. J. Snyder, who arrived in 1925 and left in 1928. Dr. F. S. Cole took over in 1929, at an annual salary of $2,000. He seems to have been still in Inlet in 1945, as it was he who was health officer when the water was labeled unsanitary.

* * *

On August 24, 1916, the Board of Health appointed William Payne as special sanitary officer at five dollars per day to guard the entrance to Eagle Bay as the area was quarantined because of the polio epidemic.

* * *

The first telephone came to Inlet in 1886.

* * *

Electricity found its way into Inlet on April 27, 1922.

* * *

Robert (Red) Rarick, the son of Arthur and Ella Rarick of the marina, was Inlet's entire summer police force until his death in the early sixties.

-7-

Roads

*I*t has been difficult for me to establish when any of the roads accessing Inlet were built. Although they were a topic of great concern in all the early records, statements are vague as to exactly where they went, and whether they were paved or just dirt. There seems to have been an unpaved road from Old Forge to Eagle Bay early on, because Marylee Armour states in her book, *Heartwood*, "In 1885, the only road to Fourth Lake was a wagon road along the North Shore of the Fulton Chain of Lakes," but I can find no record of when it was cut through. People on the South Shore had only water access to their properties until 1922, when the South Shore Road was opened. In 1926, the North Shore was paved as far as Eagle Bay, but by 1917 it must have been passable for cars as a dirt road, because Armour's father was killed while making their driveway automobile accessible.

There are references in the *History of Hamilton County* and in Frank Tiffany's diaries about a road being approved for Inlet in 1900 and of money being paid for its construction. At a Morehouse town meeting on May 18, 1901, a motion was carried that authorized the cutting of a road from Eagle Bay to Sixth Lake.

On April 3, 1902, at a special town meeting, Inlet decided to spend $8,000 to finish the highway between Sixth Lake Dam and Durant Road. Then on July 18, 1902, twenty-four voters agreed to

Looking up the Inlet.

Iron bridge across the inlet

highway taxation to build a road from Eagle Bay to Sixth Lake
Dam, for an amount not to exceed $10,000. As soon as work was
started, the dissension that seemed to plague the town when any
major project was underway arose yet again with Wellington
Kenwell suing Frank Tiffany, Supervisor; Fred Kirch, Robert
Wallace, and Fred Woolsleger, Commissioners of Highway; and
Charles O'Hara, Town Clerk, for not letting the contract to the
lowest bidder. Charles Swanson had bid $6,150 on the road,
Sperry, $6,874, and John O'Hara, $7,575. Instead of hiring the
lowest bidder, the town let the contract to O'Hara and the
Rochester Bridge and Construction Company. They were finally
exonerated of any collusion or fraud, and work continued.

Repairs for the Eagle Bay–Sixth Lake road were authorized in
1904, as was an engineer to survey a road from Sixth Lake Dam to
Seventh Lake. Then in 1907, money was allotted for road work
from Eagle Bay to Pitcher Pond, from Hess Camp to Fifth Lake,
and from Fifth Lake to the Sixth Lake Dam, as well as from the
church to the county line. (Perhaps this was on the South Shore.)
According to my grandfather's diary, on October 23, 1904, a sixty-
foot iron bridge was authorized over the inlet between the church
and the head of Fourth Lake. This puzzles me as I know of no
church that existed at that time near the inlet. I suppose that is
where the present bridge crosses by the marina.

In 1908, a road was petitioned from the Sixth Lake Dam to Limekiln Lake. This time it was the contractor, John Nelson, who sued the town before the road was completed in 1917.

We know that in 1918 a road was being constructed from Eagle Bay to Inlet, because Sue Beck's great grandfather, Edwin Harwood, was killed while trying to blast for the road. As Sue tells the story, the road crew set the dynamite charges by "biting" and crimping the caps, then, after making sure the area was cleared of people, went to Rocky Point and ate while the explosions occurred. These could be clearly heard from the hotel. When they noticed a disruption in the series of blasts, Harwood suspected a malfunction and went to investigate. When the other workmen followed, they found him dead, killed by an explosion. *The History of Hamilton County* states "roads had ceased to be troublesome to the town by the 1930s. The main highway through the area was completed, and in 1935 the Inlet–Limekiln road of 2.25 miles was added to the county highway system."

The minutes of the Seventh Lake association of August 17, 1940, note the amount of traffic congestion between the Catholic

Eagle Bay–Sixth Lake Road

Bridge by Fifth Lake

church and Mary's Gift Shop. They also document concern about the sharp curve and narrow bridge over the Sixth Lake Dam.

My family, too, had reason to be concerned. I remember this old bridge crossing the Sixth Lake outlet. I believe there was a wide curve just before the bridge, and the bridge was so narrow that cars could cross from only one direction at a time. I suppose the reason I remember it is that my father and a driver coming from the other direction ran into each other while I was in the car. Though no one was hurt, the bridge always seemed to be a hazard.

The photo on the next page of the then "new" bridge crossing the outlet between Fifth and Sixth Lakes was taken in 1920. The road followed the route of the present canoe carry toward Sixth Lake Dam and curved around to pass beside the large building, which was a welding shop and has been remodeled into the present-day home of Don and Jean Bird. This bridge was dismantled in 1944.

Although I have found records that state that a road was cut through the South Shore in 1922, there must have been some road before that, at least on the northern end, because the plaque on the bridge crossing the channel between Fifth and Sixth Lakes is dated 1903. This road passed from near where the Easy Mart now stands on Route 28, across the channel between Fifth and Sixth Lakes, through Fern Park, and out onto what is now the South Shore Road, by Tiffany Place. It then continued to Third Lake. (The plaque was

The bridge crossing the outlet between Fifth and Sixth Lakes

removed when the bridge was in danger of being replaced and it was felt a valuable landmark would be lost.) Interestingly, the road bypassed the center of Inlet. Thus, the path or sidewalk that followed the shore of Fourth Lake from Holl's Inn to the footbridge across the mouth of the inlet seems to have been the most commonly used way to town for people living in that area.

The South Shore Road was still unpaved in 1925 north of the Adirondack League Club. In 1927–28, rough grading was completed on the road from Inlet to Raquette Lake. Prior to this, people traveled the Uncas Road when it was passable due to snow conditions.

Plaque from Fifth Lake bridge

- 8 -

Private Residences

*I*nlet was speedily growing, and more and more private residences were being built, some of them very luxurious. One of the better know is the Albedor. Many stories have been written about the estate, its original owners, and the sisters for whom it was named. The information in this section comes lovingly from one who shared the joys of this beautiful summer home with her sisters and parents. She is Betty Simmons Fenton. Here is her story:

Growing up in New York City and as head of the Simmons-Boardman Publishing Company, Colonel E. Simmons felt the need for a home in the country for his family's summer vacations and his own relaxation. Friendship with O. M. Edwards and Mrs. Simmons' happy summers at Big Moose during her youth, gave Colonel Simmons and his wife, Ida, the inspiration to choose beautiful Fourth Lake as the likely spot on which to build their summer estate.

Under the architectural plans of Mrs. Simmons, construction was started in 1927 and completed in 1928. Named for their three daughters, Aline, Betty, and Doris, Albedor spread over many acres and contained many buildings other than the main house: a laundry, icehouse,

Albedor

Albedor Boathouse

garage with an apartment for the caretaker, and also a tennis court. The best area of all though, was the playground with three life-size playhouses, complete with sanitary and cooking facilities, where three girls could even entertain adults at (grown-up) tables and chairs. Not to be forgotten was the play store, the Albedor Supply, which sold miniature replicas of all the national brand products with sales rung up on a tiny cash register which actually worked.

Wintertime fun was not neglected, as a toboggan slide was erected on the opposite side of the property from the playground and many brisk hours were spent snowshoeing on frozen Fourth Lake.

After the main house was completed, attention was turned to the boathouse, which boasted a huge entire second floor room for dancing and entertainment, complete with stage. In 1931, the Colonel and his wife were making plans for an anniversary celebration in October, but his death in September of that year put an end to any festivities. Mrs. Simmons carried on at the estate alone and, in 1936, put her architectural talents to use once again by having another home constructed on the property for her oldest daughter, Aline, who was then married and the mother of two.

Faced with the rising costs and children not able to spend time with her during the summers, in 1950 Mrs. Simmons reluctantly decided to sell Albedor. Unfortunately, she passed away September 20, 1951, so did not live to meet any new owners. The estate was willed to a Brooklyn Orphan Asylum, which in turn sold it to private owners, of whom over the years there were several, until Mr. And Mrs. Hans Holl purchased Albedor [in 1956] and turned it into a charming hotel. [The Albedor is now a private residence.]

As to the namesakes of Albedor, Aline was struck by a car in Orlando, Florida, and killed instantly on November 22, 1963, the day of the Kennedy assassination. Doris is now Mrs. Fred Hatter and resides in Melbourne, Florida, and Betty has a home on Third Lake.

An early brochure advertising the property for sale tells that

Albedor was built on twenty-eight acres. The cost to build it in 1927 through 1928 was $500,000. The main lodge contains twenty big rooms. The living room extends sixty-five feet along the front of the building; its huge picture windows give a panoramic view of Fourth Lake. The main entrance hall is thirty feet square and finished in red fir. The stairway has sweeping bark-covered rails. The living room fireplace is ten feet wide, composed of only thirteen stones, all hammered by hand from a large boulder found on the estate, and it accommodates five-foot long logs. The stone mantel shelf is a single piece, over twelve feet long and weighing two tons. There are five and a half miles of plumbing, sixteen miles of wiring, and a hundred tons of slate in the roof of the building.

Paownyc

Perhaps many readers remember, as I do, dancing in the room over the boathouse to the music of a small orchestra after the Holls purchased Albedor.

Another luxurious estate located on the north shore of Fourth Lake is Paownyc. O.M. Edwards, whose father had been very successful with his department stores, added to the wealth of the family by inventing folding railroad-car steps and the mechanism to raise and lower car windows. He named his camp Paownyc for the three railroads that contributed so much to his wealth: "Pa" for Pennsylvania Railroad, "ow" for Ohio and Western, and "nyc" for New York Central.

This estate is also comprised of several buildings, including a large boathouse with beautiful living quarters above, majestic fireplaces, and hidden passageways.

One of the oldest camps still in existence is the Spencer Camp, built on the corner of the inlet facing down the lake across from the Arrowhead property. The two-story camp was built about 1894, with half-log bark siding on the exterior. This siding, made of winter-cut, bug-free black spruce so that it would retain its bark, has survived more than one hundred years. On the hillside above, there is a unique, small cottage added around 1921. A steep hill runs from the road down to the camp, and since there was no road access at the time it was built, the Spencer family used a pulley and

Spencer Camp   *Highland Lodge*

basket to transport goods down to the building. Though it was built quite close to the water, trees grew so thickly around the camp that it could not be seen from the lake. I remember Sally Spencer Clump, a famous singer in her day, vacationing here in the summer. The camp still stands, much of it in its original state, though now a driveway connects it to the main road and many of the trees have been cut.

Another early camp was Highland Lodge, built around 1895 by Dwight Sperry. In 1896, he sold it to Angeline Bailey and used the money to build the Eagle Bay Hotel. In 1920, Philo Wood bought the camp, which adjoined his Wood Hotel property. It is now privately owned.

Charles Pratt, petroleum pioneer and co-founder of Standard Oil Company, owned the first camp on the south shore of Fourth Lake near Inlet, which was built about where Holl's Inn is today.

Although far from possessing the splendor of the preceding camps, Kirch Camp has the distinction of being the second one built on the south shore, and it is still in use as a private camp today. It was built by my father, Fred Kirch, around 1894. The *Utica Daily Press* stated on Thursday morning, August 9, 1894, that:

> Fred Kirch has one of the prettiest camps on Fourth Lake. High and dry, on a decided elevation, with a charming view of the lake, it makes a most inviting place. Fred has accommodations for ten.

Crosswinds now occupies the site where Arthur Rarick once had his home and business, a marine service station. One of his services

Kirch Camp

utilized a railroad track that ran down into the water. A train car could run down the track, load on a big steamboat, pull it out for servicing, then return it to the lake. The property included a beautiful and extensive sand beach and a view down the length of Fourth Lake to exquisite sunsets.

A long, rather narrow dock stretched out into the lake, and back in the trees was the Raricks' home. This spot holds precious memories

Arthur Rarick's Marine Service Station (Boats were not the only vehicles serviced by the marina. Here you can see an early bi-plane being refueled. Seaplanes have long been noticeable in the area and have served to take fishermen and hunters to remote locations, transport people from the cities to the camps, provide scenic flights, and conduct fire runs over the woods.)

for me, for it was here that I stayed in the Adirondacks for the first five summers of my life. My family rented the house, while the Raricks moved into the apartment above the boathouse. There was a lean-to on the little stream that flowed into the lake near the house, which was reached by a path through the cedar trees that grew thickly around it. It seemed such an adventure to a small child to walk to this lean-to, though looking at the area now that it has been cleared, it seems there could never have been room for the seemingly long walk that I remember taking as a small child. I am always brought back to that spot by the smell of cedar.

I will digress from the stories of Inlet to tell the most vivid experience I remember while staying at the Rarick's. My father continued working through the summers and came from Watertown to join us at camp only on weekends. One Sunday morning, my sister and I were dressed early for church and persuaded our father to let us walk out on the dock with him. The Raricks owned a large, very friendly collie dog who was always delighted to see us. That morning, spotting us on

My sisters Eleanor and Marion, and me, with Rex

the dock, he came bounding down to greet us, knocking both my sister and me into the lake. I must have been three years old at the time, and my sister, five. Though he was dressed in his best and only Sunday clothes, my father hesitated only a moment before he jumped in to rescue us. I don't know why I have kept such a vivid memory of this, as I was not scared in the least, but seem to remember thinking that I would float over to my grandfather's home across the lake.

Harold's log cabin

Another lovely, early camp was Naumkeag, located just a short distance down the South Shore Road. I will let one of the present owners, Barbara Norkus, tell of its interesting beginning:

In the summer of 1913, Harold V. Nielsen, age 12, worked on a special project while he spent the summer in Inlet with his parents and older sister, Florence. At the end of the summer, Harold took his father, Andrew, down South Shore Road about a quarter of a mile from Inlet, to show his father the fruits of his summer-long labor. It was a one-room log cabin, complete with a door and window. He flatly stated that this was the perfect spot to build a summer home. Andrew apparently agreed, as he bought the lot, actually two lots because Harold had built the cabin right on the line.

A summer home with a front and back porch, living room, den, and half bath was built. There were also three bedrooms and a bathroom upstairs. When Florence married Carter Goodrich, Andrew built a home for them next door. Then, when Harold married Charlotte Smith, Andrew added to his own home, a sunroom and dining room downstairs, as well as two bedrooms and a bath upstairs, knowing Harold would be inheriting this house.

While Harold was working on his log cabin, he chose the name Naumkeag, an Indian word meaning, "a quiet

Original Naumkeag

Boathouse at Naumkeag with house in background

resting place by the water." His house has always been called by this name, and the pillars on the South Shore Road have plates imbedded in the rocks with Naumkeag imprinted thereon. Florence's house eventually became known as "Little Naumkeag."

Andrew also built a larger garage at the far side of the property which was converted to a cottage called "Shintangle" when Florence inherited that piece of property along with the property on which her house was built. Harold inherited the middle portion of the entire property, which included a single slip boathouse.

In 1942, Harold replaced this with a four-slip boathouse with two recreation rooms on the second floor. These were very popular places with both the older and the younger generations for years to come.

Harold's daughter, Barbara, and her husband, Raymond Norkus, live in Naumkeag for most of the year. Their hope is to preserve, as much as possible, the buildings and their uniqueness in this ever-changing world. The log cabin, which started it all, can still be seen from the South Shore Road during late fall, winter, and spring.

All of the places were not so luxurious. Although south of the Inlet border, I could not resist including this picture of an early Minnow Brook Camp. At this time, it was a private camp, and not the elaborate lodging place it was to become.

Minnow Brook Camp

-9-

Personal Reminiscences

$\mathcal{W}$e will leave the buildings of the time to learn about some of the people who lived in them. I am sure each one would have an interesting story to tell if we could but talk to them. Here follow a few of their stories, some told to me, others written down by the people who lived them. I start with a short memoir of my grandfather as I wrote it some time ago, much of it gleaned from his faithfully-kept diaries. As he was one of the early settlers and the first town supervisor, it seems a fitting place to begin.

January 14, 1902, was a very cold day, with temperatures of fifteen below zero, according to the diary of my grandfather, Frank Tiffany, who on that day was elected the first town supervisor of the newly established Town of Inlet. "There were 35 votes cast, no opposition," he notes. He was to hold this position for the next twenty-five years. Frank was born in Grieg, New York in 1863. There he married Ida Puffer, who gave birth to a daughter Lettie Mae in 1889, then died of "consumption" (tuberculosis) when the baby was about nine months old. In 1892, Frank left the young child with his mother and an unmarried sister and sought a new life in the Adirondacks.

Three years later, he married Anna Kirch, also from Grieg, to which union a son Lansing was born, and Frank soon brought his new family to settle in Inlet. He had come to this area at the urging

Frank Tiffany   *Fred Kirch*

of my father Fred Kirch who had left his home in Grieg at the age of thirteen and followed the Independence and Moose Rivers on foot to Big Moose, looking for a better life than he was sharing with seven siblings on a farm that "wouldn't grow white beans." Here he found a wilderness that he felt was full of opportunities, and he persuaded many others from Lewis County to join him. Among them, besides some of his siblings, were Roy Rogers, Charlie O'Hara, and the Delmarshes, all of whom stayed to become prominent members of the developing community of Inlet.

In the course of his years here, Fred worked in many capacities, but during that first winter in the Adirondacks, he was employed to stay on Cedar Island to protect it from being taken back by the state from people who had claimed it by "squatter's rights." He later worked in lumber camps, was a steamboat operator, guided hunting parties, and served as fire warden and highway superintendent. On one memorable occasion, he was hired with Arch Delmarsh to transport a woman with tuberculosis to a remote hotel inaccessible by road. She couldn't walk, so they took turns carrying her in a chair strapped to their backs. He also corralled deer to be moved to

Pennsylvania and helped build camps for the rich and famous. One of his favorite stories features Will Durant, who asked if he could construct a circular stairway. Fred replied in the affirmative, though he knew little about building any kind of stair, but he did complete it satisfactorily.

In 1899, he started a steamboat company that would transport passengers and provisions up through the Fulton Chain from Old Forge to the luxurious, but nearly inaccessible, camps further to the north. Frank notes in his diary that "Kirch's new steamboat made its first trip on July 22, 1899." Although a successful venture at the time, the coming of extended train services and the improvement of roads made this manner of transportation outmoded, and Fred moved on to other ventures.

In 1903, as road commissioner, he was instrumental in building the old iron bridge which spans the channel between Fifth and Sixth Lakes. At that time, the road led from the South Shore Road through the Loomis Field, then known as Fern Park, to meet what is now Route 28 above Fifth Lake. The plaque with his name on it remained on the bridge, marking it as a special place for his descendants to picnic and reminisce, until the town threatened to raze the bridge due to its deteriorating condition. At this point, one of the enterprising descendants had the plaque removed, mounted, and presented to an astounded mother, as a very unusual but much appreciated Christmas present. However, the bridge was repaired to be used as a snowmobile crossing, so it can still be visited by younger generations.

Although Fred left the area shortly after this, Frank Tiffany stayed to become a permanent a contributing resident of Inlet for the rest of his life. While he was building a house for his family, his wife and son spent much time at their home in Grieg. Frank mentions getting a letter from Anna saying that all were well. He records in his diary that day, "I like to get such news, but wish I could be with my family all the time."

Although the home that Tiffany built has had several renovations, the main building still looks much as it did when he and Anna lived there. The back part, containing an icehouse, summer kitchen, woodshed, etc., was lost in a fire many years ago.

I have few actual memories of my grandfather, as he died when I was very young, but from his diaries, the stories told by relatives, and the pictures and mementoes found in his home, which is still

*Frank Tiffany's house on Fourth Lake, now owned by Jeff Haynes.
(Notice the sidewalk. I have been told that it ran along the shore from
at least the Neodak Hotel to the footbridge crossing the Inlet by the
Arrowhead Hotel and served as a public walkway.)*

in our family, I have a vivid picture of this man who was so instrumental in the founding of Inlet.

These carefully kept diaries are a great treasure of information about life in those days. Foremost in all of the entries was discussion of the weather, a factor so important to maintaining life in this remote area that it superseded even references to the wars. So, buried in among "cold last night," and "fair winter day," was the brief entry, "Lansing [his son] started for Utica to enlist." He does mention on May 2, 1898, a "great naval battle in the Philippine Isles. U.S. Navy achieves a glorious victory by Commodore Dewey. Spaniards sustain a terrible defeat" and on June 21, 1900, records how "McKinley and Roosevelt were nominated by acclamation." On November 11, 1918, he wrote that he "arrived in Utica just before 3 o'clock this A.M. Had just gone to bed when the city hall bell began ringing. I dressed and went down on the street and learned that the peace armistice had been signed. Soon the crowd assembled and the noise and confusion continued until midnight."

On New Years Day 1902, Frank writes that he "cut wood with Frank Loson on Hess's lot to fill his shed," and on February 2 he notes, "bear did not see his shadow." There are many references to the extremely cold days, though these did not seem to deter him from his work. At temperatures of twenty below zero, he was building a dock. References to the cold continue:

"Ice about 30 inches thick."

"Snowshoeing the worst I have ever experienced."

"Thawed out water pipes."

"Shoveled snow from roof of upper camp."

And on April 19, "ice gone from the lake."

Warmer temperatures brought other problems, as evidenced by his note that says, "got stuck in the mud just below Eagle Bay on the way home." He "sowed sweet peas, lettuce this forenoon in upper garden," one year in March, when weather was "much warmer today." He always maintained an unfenced, beautiful garden. Today I wonder how he kept the deer from eating everything, but potato bugs were a problem then as now, for one thing I do remember is picking them off his plants as a little girl. As the season progressed, he reports, "flies, mosquitoes, and punkies make life miserable," and on June 23, that it snowed.

One of the necessary activities that consumed much of everyone's time in those days was the cutting of ice. My grandfather, according to his diaries, spent day after day filling neighbors' icehouses.

The pages are filled with names of the early settlers: "filled Charlie's [O'Hara] icehouse with 700 cakes, 14 inches thick;" "helped George Rarick fill Mohawk icehouse;" and "shoveled sawdust for Archie's [Delmarsh] icehouse." He also spent much time cutting and hauling wood, and painting boats, buildings, and fences.

Although these photographs were taken recently, the machine pictured is one of the originals used to cut ice, and it is still used today on the one occasion each year when the old tradition is re-enacted in Raquette Lake.

An old ice-cutting machine

Ice-cutting on Raquette Lake

But life during that time was not all work and no play. Those early settlers often met for entertainment, though not what we would probably do today. They spent much time "visiting," and that is exactly what they did—talk. I remember lying in bed as a child, listening to the conversations going on downstairs, to the stories told, and most especially, to the accompanying laughter. I also remember being taken on these "visits," usually on Sunday afternoons, occasions where we children sat silently while the grown-ups talked. I don't remember minding this, maybe because it was an accepted way of life. I remember that at one house there was a furry, stuffed cat I was allowed to hold to help pass the time, and that at another I was intrigued by a paperweight with a turtle with legs that wiggled.

However, the town's early settlers certainly enjoyed livelier times as well, and they would walk many miles to enjoy a dance. During 1902, Frank went to a card party at George Delmarsh's on February 8, to a party at Kenwell's on February 14, and on April 11, he went dancing at O'Hara's. He often mentions going to tea at someone's home and playing cards on Cedar Island with the Delmarshes. He also enjoyed ice skating parties and listening to phonographs, and picnics were a popular form of entertainment. One unfortunate day, he went to Bubb's Lake for a pancake dinner and on the way home was caught in a wind and rain storm.

Many of the stories and many pages of Frank's diaries are concerned with his trips, since it was so very difficult to get from one place to another in those days, and his very active political life required him to travel often. To go almost anywhere, he first had to go to Eagle Bay, often rowing or walking, sometimes across the ice. He tells of one spring day when he tried to cross with a team of horses and the ice was so thin, "that we singled the horses out and drove one ahead of the other." Not willing to risk the trip back, they left the horses there and walked back to Hess's. In spite of his frequent travels, Frank had lived in Inlet seven years before he saw Limekiln Lake, and that was the same year he finally made it to Blue Mountain. That was a trip that took him eight hours to go one way. A few pages later he records that he went again, and made it in six hours. It was another fifteen years before he made it to Indian Lake.

Frank's business often called him to Lake Pleasant, the county seat, a trip which could take him three days, though it was only about forty miles as the crow flies. He would first go to Old Forge, often by foot (a two and a half hour walk) if he could not catch a ride, then take a train to Utica, change for Albany, then go to Northville, to Wells, and finally, Lake Pleasant. Often returning after dark, he crossed the ice from Eagle Bay to his home on the South Shore by the light of shavings burning in a frying pan he carried. There was no road from Eagle Bay to Inlet at that time, nor a passage up the South Shore from Old Forge. Sometimes he pulled Anna, his wife, on a sled across the ice to Rocky Point.

An example of one of Frank's trips is recorded on March 21, 1899: He departed after a meeting in Morehouse and "started for Remsen about 8:00 P.M. Arrived there at 2:00 A.M.. Left at 3:00, arrived Fulton Chain (Thendara), 4:00 A.M. Started for Inlet 9:00 A.M. Arrived 2:00 P.M.—drew wood rest of afternoon." It's no wonder that he worked so energetically for improved roads.

It would seem that holidays were not much cause for celebration, or even for varying the work schedule. On one Thanksgiving he worked for Arch Delmarsh, "drawing dirt for Pratt's croquet ground," on another, "plastered in the kitchen," and yet another, "started digging a well." One Christmas he "shingled in forenoon on Frankie's building with the other boys," but he did at times go somewhere for Christmas dinner. He must have wanted to observe Sunday as a day of rest, however, as he records one Sunday after he finished filling someone's icehouse, that he was, "very much dissatisfied to work on Sunday."

Diseases were different then, or at least called by other names, and were much more serious than in these days of antibiotics and vaccinations. Frank's son was often noted to be "sick with the grippe." Frank also tells of someone dying of "consumption at Hess's." In those days when infantile paralysis was so deadly and so prevalent, Inlet took the precaution of placing all children sixteen years old or younger who were coming from infected areas under quarantine for two weeks. Tragically, and somewhat needlessly, Frank's own young wife died in 1918. She developed appendicitis, and the doctors were so swamped with patients suffering from the influenza epidemic that was raging at the time that they did not get to remove her infected appendix before it ruptured. She died a few days later from peritonitis. She had been in a hospital in Utica, and Frank records coming home to Inlet that day, "but not such a home as it was a few days ago." Lansing (Frank's son) was in the Navy serving on a battleship at the time, but was given a short leave to come home.

On a happier note, Frank Tiffany records getting his first automobile earlier that year. He writes, "took automobile out of garage alone and ran it up to ball ground [¼ mile] and back twice which was very good for the first time." Of course, no driving license was required at the time.

Frank Tiffany with his car

122. Inlet Inn, Head of Fourth Lake, Fulton Chain, Adirondack Mts.

The footbridge built by Frank Tiffany

Frank worked at many trades during the course of his life. Given his slight build, it's a wonder that he could survive the rigor and hardships he so frequently faced. He guided hunting parties, packing boats and equipment through the woods to remote areas. He painted, cut wood and ice, hauled boulders for foundations and docks (as the huge ones supporting his house attest), did surveying, was assessor and notary, fought forest fires, and worked on construction. On July 18, 1902, he mentions commencing to build the footbridge across the inlet by the old Arrowhead Hotel, which shows up in many of the old pictures.

In 1915, Frank established a real estate and insurance business which is still in operation today under the name of Burkhard-Evans. He was trustee of the school, and served on the board of the Old Forge Bank. After twenty-five years as Supervisor of the Town of Inlet, he was elected County Judge.

A newspaper article of the day records:

> Election is once more over and our little hamlet is as quiet and peaceful as though nothing had happened. But we sure did have an interesting time on election day. The

main thing that gave interest to our voting was the fact
that our popular supervisor, F.E. Tiffany was a candidate
for county judge and that he won out is very gratifying to
his hosts of friends. Mr. Tiffany has served our town as
supervisor for twenty-five years, being the first one to
hold that office and having been re-elected every year
since. The faithful service that he has rendered makes a
record of which his friends are proud and we feel that
nothing more be said as that "speaks for itself." His
friends are pleased that his new office will not take him
away from us but that he will remain in Inlet.

It continues:

> Mr. Tiffany carried Hamilton County by 200 majority
> over his opponent, Henry D. Kellogg of Long Lake.

The bitter quarrels that eventually ensued over attempts to
install a public water system to service the rapidly growing town
are not recorded in Frank's diaries. This part of the story I heard
from my mother, who, with tears filling her eyes, recounted how
hard he fought and worked for this benefit to Inlet. Opposed by the
new supervisor who owned the private water system, C.F. Lee, and
faced with the stress of opposing some of his lifelong friends and
neighbors, Frank's heart could not withstand all the years of hard
work, and he died in 1931, the water problem unsolved, as it
remains to the present day.

My mother was Frank's daughter by his first wife, Ida. For his
second wife, Frank chose Anna Kirch, who was a sister to Fred
Kirch, so when Fred eventually married my mother, he was marry-
ing his niece by marriage. Though some fifteen years older than his
wife, they had a wonderfully happy union. Through them, I have
had access to much of the history of Inlet, passed down to me from
both sides of my family.

In 1924, Frank's son Lansing married Magdelene Kopp of
Utica, whom he had met while she was on vacation at Rocky Point,
where he was employed. They had eight children. What follows
was written by their eldest daughter, Beverly Tiffany Joslin:

> Frank Tiffany was my grandfather and married Anna
> Kirch, sister of Laura Kirch Delmarsh. He had two wives,

Ida Puffer, mother of Lettie Tiffany, and Anna Kirch, who was the mother of Lansing Tiffany who was my father. Frank owned property next to the Neodak and also came from Greig. He built the large house on the lake and a smaller one nearer the road (which was not there then). In his writing at one time he told about going across the ice to Rocky Point, drawing Anna on a sled, for Sunday dinners.

Anna died in 1917 while my father was in college. He was one of the first ones from the area to attend college (Holy Cross College).

He joined the Navy, but was deferred until gradua-tion. He finally got on a ship for Europe, but the ship was torpedoed. They returned to the U.S. for repairs, but the war ended before the ship was repaired. He served three years in the Navy, but that was all he saw of the war.

He and his wife settled in Inlet, living with Frank before moving to a house of their own on the South Shore Road that Lansing had built for them.

Frank and Lansing Tiffany

The Post Office building was owned early on by Frank and then Lansing as they had an insurance business on the second floor. They were both Hamilton County judges. In 1936, Lansing and his family moved to Long Island where he worked for the Brooklyn Edison Company. When World War II started in 1944, they returned to Inlet and with K. Leonard Harwood opened the Inlet Appliance Store, orig-inally the Inlet Supply owned by Floyd Puffer. They resumed life in the home they had kept on the South Shore Rd.

Beverly goes on to reminisce about her own life:

As a child growing up in Inlet, many of my memories are of the school which was in the same building as it is now. There were eight grades at that time. Most of the children went to Raquette Lake for high school, with a few going to Old Forge. The students who went to Old Forge had to live with a relative there. The original little schoolhouse building was used only for voting purposes. There was no kindergarten at that time, and there were three teachers for the eight grades. Marion Puffer, who lived next door to the school, taught 1st and 2nd grades. Eleanor Buckley taught 3rd, 4th, and 5th, and Blanche Rupert taught 6th, 7th, and 8th.

Miss Buckley and Miss Rupert boarded at the home of Roy Rogers who was the owner of the Neodak Hotel. Miss Rupert was not very well liked by the students. She had a car, but would not give Miss Buckley a ride to school. As a result, Miss Buckley walked along with Charlie Barker, Dr. Jones's two children, the Fredettes, the Meneillys, and myself. One time when we were on lunch break, the boys got together and piled snow around Miss Rupert's back tires. The girls helped them get water and pour it on the snow. It was frozen by the time school was out. Since we all disappeared rapidly at that time, I was told she had to go to Joe Payne's gas station, which was across the road from the school, to get help getting out.

I do not recall any organizations except for the two churches in town: Church of the Lakes and St. Anthony's Catholic Church.

Dr. Cole lived in the house next to where Pedals and Petals is now. He was capable of treating a cold and fixing broken bones. Dr. Robert Lindsey, Sr. lived in Old Forge and would come to Inlet for an emergency.

The North Shore was paved, but the South Shore was sand about half way to Old Forge.

There were several very active hotels in the area at the time. In the village, Hodel's Adirondack Store was The Inlet Supply, owned by Floyd Puffer. There were two grocery stores, The Red and White, and Harry Hall's Grocery. Namtella Kalil owned the store which is now Herb Schmid's, but it was only open in the summer. These are some of my memories of Inlet in 1924–1936.

Beverly enclosed a picture of many of the school children taken at a birthday party at Harwoods.

Pictured above: Bruce Puffer, Bud Hall, Malcome Cameron, Gordon Rudd, Junior Blakeman, Teddy Harwood, Alfred Thibado, Bobby Harwood, Janet Puffer, Elizabeth Thibado, Rosemary Tiffany, Irene Blakeman, Jeanne Harwood, Norma Fredette, Beverly Tiffany, Virginia Rivette

* * *

Another Inlet resident of note is Louise Payne. She lived to be one of the oldest Inlet residents and had five children, four of whom settled in Inlet. Besides Richard Jr. and James, whom she mentions in her story, there were Sidney, Theodore, and Rosemary. Here is part of her story as taken from the *Adirondack Tourist* of February 8, 1984:

> Louise Payne is true Adirondack stock. She was born at the turn of the century in a small cabin at Sucker Brook in Raquette Lake. One of her early stories concerns a runaway horse. Her father had purchased a bicycle, and once had to rescue his bride and two young daughters when the team of horses bolted and ran away with the wagon. Apparently, he caught up with the wagon and stopped the team shortly before it reached the edge of a cliff. "A real wild west show."

After moving to California for a while, the family returned and moved to Sixth Lake near Inlet, and lived there for a short time with only a handful of neighbors. Louise said, "I remember as well as can be when the house at Sixth Lake burned. My mother was doing a big load of laundry one day, and my sister and I were helping her. We took a big basket of clothes up the stairs...the fire may have been going when we went up, but we didn't know. Mother thought she smelled smoke when she was getting dinner which was at noontime, so she went and looked."

Louise recalled that her father had applied for insurance on the house, but he was originally refused because there was no chimney. He completed the chimney, which was later suspected as the possible cause of the fire, and he had mailed the insurance papers shortly before the blaze. "He always figured the chimney wasn't built quite right. We didn't save hardly anything. They took my mother's sewing machine clear down by the lake, I remember. Of course, they didn't have a fire department then. The only way they knew if there was a fire was if someone would go and ring the church bell."

Even though many people showed up to fight the blaze, the house was a total loss. It was December, and Louise remembers that the volunteers had to chop holes in the ice and shuttle water from the lake in a bucket brigade.

"They saved the kitchen stove, I remember that," she chuckled. "Mrs. Kimmel took my mother's kettle of oyster stew and dumped it on the fire so they could move the stove." Louise's three-year-old brother considered himself one of the day's heros, proclaiming he had saved Louise's doll from the blaze. "My brother and I were great pals," Louise interjected. "He called me Weezy because he couldn't say Louise when he was small. He would always say, 'I saved Weezy's doll.'"

The family boarded for a while at Riley Johnson's, a neighbor. Louise remembers that a small shop, previously used for storage was converted into living quarters, with sheets and draperies for room dividers. It was humble and austere, but the experience illustrated the residents' concern

Louise Payne at her home in Inlet

for one another. When tragedy struck, Inlet residents banded together and provided what was necessary for their neighbors.

Her father then completed another house known as the Golf Course House, which still is in use today as the clubhouse at Deer Run Golf Course in Inlet. [This is not the case now.] He owned forty acres at the site. The previous spring, Louise remembers, her mother had trekked through the property daily collecting sap for maple syrup. "We would go out to meet her in the afternoon after school. She would take my brother sometimes, pulling him along in the sleigh. The women wore long skirts then, and I remember her dress would be ice clear up over her knees from walking in the snow."

Her mother kept a full schedule, as did all the women in the area. Louise explained that the women had a full time job keeping the house and taking care of the children, back-breaking work that was accomplished without the benefit of modern conveniences. The women in the area in the early 1900s also helped the men, who worked mainly as guides and builders. Her mother had worked alongside

Lou Porter when he built the family houses. When the children weren't attending school, they helped, too. Not for allowances or special favors, but because the family lived and worked together to accomplish whatever needed to be done.

Louise started school in Inlet when she was about seven, which was normal for the times, "Kids started school later then," she noted. "Many of the families did a lot of lessons in the home." The school she attended before 1910 remains intact today. [The smaller schoolhouse] When Louise went to school there, the classes met in one room with one teacher. She still has a picture of those early days in the one-room schoolhouse, with eight grades of 20–30 students positioned in the classroom. "My first teacher was Mary Caulfield, who later married Floyd Puffer. We all sat in the rear portion of the room, and each class would come forward to the recitation bench to do their lessons. One teacher we had for a long time was Mrs. Gebhardt, who later taught in the Thendara school. When we went to Old Forge later for Regents exams, I'd hike to Thendara to see her. [Soon major construction took place at the school, and the larger building was added.] At one time, the school went up to the tenth grade. Then the students had to go to Old Forge or somewhere else to graduate high school. There was a room downstairs where we'd play volleyball, and there was a workshop down there, too. During recess we'd quick finish our lunch and go sliding on the hill." Louise attended the school until she was 15, and the family continued to live at the Golf Course House near Limekiln Road. The family then moved to New Jersey where her father worked as a builder in the shipyards of Gloucester during World War I. They returned to Inlet after the war.

Louise's story continues in the February 22, 1984 issue of the *Adirondack Tourist*:

> Very early she [Louise] cultivated a keen sense of humor, nurtured, no doubt, by her father, Lou Porter, who she remembers as frequently roaring "with a laugh that came

up from his toes. He'd laugh until he had tears in his eyes."

As a child, Louise provided many occasions for laughter, with her quick eye and even quicker wit, which was apparently often masked by youthful naivete. Once, while traveling to "The Forge" from Inlet on one of the early steamships, Louise's mother, Esther, noticed her staring intently at a gentleman on the boat. Louise remembers that the trips down the Fulton Chain of lakes were special events and usually the scenic voyage was an adventure for the youngsters. That day, however, something else fascinated the young Louise. Noting that it was impolite to stare at someone, her mother implored Louise to stop. "But Mother," the youngster explained loudly, "he looks just like a bulldog!"

On a trip to Utica when she was a child, she was obviously amazed at the development of the urban area. It should have been expected, for, as she explains now, "Every place with more than six houses was a city." Her father took her to Utica to meet her sister, and the three were making their way through the canal area when Lou Porter admonished Louise for not watching where she was going. Admittedly, Louise now says, she was amply awed by the city, and was "rubber-necking" to take in all the sights. "Louise," her father warned, "watch where you're going or you'll run into something." "But Papa," she said with a straight face, "I'm only taking one step at a time."

She grew up during a time when travel to Old Forge meant a lengthy trip by steamboat in the summer, or a ride on the mail sleigh in the winter. There was no road through Inlet at the time, and the tourists who came to the tiny hamlet nestled in the mountains at the end of Fourth Lake, came by steamboat or train. "Most of the hotels," Louise explained, "provided stage-coaches and other overland transportation for their guests. The people would come into Eagle Bay on the train, and then up to Inlet on the stage-coach."

"In the summer, travelers would take the train from Eagle Bay to Raquette Lake, then board the steamers to Marion River. We would ride that tiny railroad shuttle there," she said, "the Marion River carry. There were no sides on the train, as I remember. I would sit on those cane seats, and I was so short, my feet wouldn't touch the floor." It was a terrifying experience for a young girl, one that she remembers to this day. "My sister was taller, and she could brace her feet on the seat in front of her. I kept sliding off the cane seat, and I was afraid I was going to slide right off the train." Once safely deposited in Blue Mountain Lake by steamboat, Louise knew the trip to Indian Lake to visit relatives meant another long journey by stage-coach.

Louise remembers the Inlet of her youth as a small, bustling community, centered around the tourist hotels and the lumber industry. "The big hotels like the Wood Hotel, the Arrowhead, and the Seventh Lake House were all busy then," she recalls, "and Rocky Point and the Parquet did very well. One of our favorite places was the covered walkway at the Wood Hotel, where the stage-coaches would pull up to let their passengers off."

"Then, as now, the locals often provided life's color," she explained. "Once," she remembers, "a young female tourist ventured into town from one of the hotels in search of the famous and elusive 'lumberjack.' The young lady inquired at Kimmel's where she might find some lumber-jacks, because she was anxious to see what they looked like. According to Louise, Kimmel pointed toward the bay of Fifth Lake where some lumbermen were grouping logs in the water. 'Well look right down there,' he boomed. 'There they are.' 'Well, they look just like men!' exclaimed the surprised visitor. I can't imagine what she was expecting," Louise laughed.

Her own recreation during her childhood was centered mostly around the family. Picnics and outings were a favorite pass time of the Porters. Louise's father, an accomplished outdoorsman, led local excursions to Seventh and Eighth Lakes, and Black Bear Mountain. She remembers picnicking near Battleship Rock, a boulder near the Seventh Lake bridge that they named. The bridge, she noted, had been there in one form or another for as long as she could recall.

Louise also remembers the early dam at Sixth Lake,

Road over Sixth Lake Dam

which was flat across the top, without handrails. "I used to be petrified of that dam," she said. "I always worried about falling off the walkway into the water."

Later she spent much time on the water in the "Green Devil," a boat built by her father. "He would come down the lake singing at the top of his lungs, La-de da-de-da. Everyone would always say, 'Well, here comes Lou Porter.' Sometimes he took the family around Fourth Lake, or down to Old Forge. There was a bakery down there, and we would always go to the French bakery for treats"

At home, evenings were spent listening to her father read from his treasured collection of famous books. "He had the entire collection of 'Tarzan and the Apes' and the old Cape Cod stories," she said smiling. "In the winter, Dad would read all the time. We'd hurry home from school, and we'd hurry with our homework and the dishes to listen to him."

"The big social events," Louise fondly recalls, "were the dances and card parties held at the hotels." There again, the entire family participated, and Louise regards that spirit of togetherness and involvement in all activities, a main ingredient of the solid Adirondack heritage.

Louise was no stranger to hard work, and she paid her dues in local employment before the family moved to

New Jersey during World War I. She had worked at the local ice cream parlor, and went with her older sister once, and only once, to wait on tables at the Parquet. "I didn't know anything about waiting on tables, except what we did in our home," she exclaimed, "and they didn't tell me anything either. They just sent me out there. We were supposed to get some plates from the other room to serve the soup on. Well, I just put the soup bowls right on the table...I didn't know. In our house, if you had plates there, you put the soup on them, if not, then you put the soup bowls right on the table. Mrs. Parquet went right up one side of me and down the other," Louise laughed. "I said then and there I would never wait on table again. And I never have since, either."

Louise and her family then moved to New Jersey for a short time while her father worked in the shipyards of Gloucester. She left behind the memories of the pickle boat that used to deliver supplies around the lake, and the memories of her trips with her mother down the very rugged and newly opened South Shore Road.

When she returned a few short years later, she found many more people and automobiles that traveled about in winter, a feat previously unthought of in the area, due in large part to the conditions of the roads and the cars. The Limekiln road was finished, and the outlying areas of Inlet were beginning to show life in the form of year-round residents.

The road from Eagle Bay was completely relaid and refinished in the early 1920s, and Inlet was readily accessible.

Finding little work in the area except the resort related waitress jobs she had previously disavowed, Louise went to Utica, and found work in a knitting mill. She remained there until she was married in Utica in 1925 to Richard Payne of Raquette Lake.

Richard, a builder by trade, took his bride to Florida, where Louise gave birth to the first of her five children, Richard Jr. She said she really didn't enjoy Florida too much, and she was troubled by the prejudices of many of the southern people. "They said you weren't supposed to turn out for the 'coloreds' or the 'Georgia crackers' but I didn't see anything wrong with the folks. We didn't turn out for them especially. For a time we had some 'Georgia crackers' living with us, and they were nice people."

Then, reminiscent of her father's travels, the Paynes moved back to Inlet briefly, and then were off to again to California. Another son, James, was born in California, and the two babies kept Louise very busy working at home while Richard was busy working as a contractor.

A short time afterwards, the Adirondack natives traded their sand flies for black flies, and returned for the last time to settle in Inlet. The transition wasn't accomplished witout effort. Louise even had to re-learn her native tongue. "I was used to saying fawg for fog, and other things," she drawled. "I got used to saying some things so people out there wouldn't laugh at me. Then I had to change them around again."

The old values and the basic lifestyle remained, however, and soon the Paynes had forged a small farm out of the Inlet countryside near Limekiln Road, where Richard Jr. now lives. There was nothing unusual about having a cow for milk and other dairy products. Louise's family had always had a cow. The horse, pigs, and chickens were very natural to self-sufficient Adirondackers, as well. Louise grew the family's vegetables and produce in a large garden by the house, and when one of the boys became interested in raising turkeys, the farm produced a record 25-pounder. "The eggs we didn't use we sold to the Hurley and Ryan Grocery Store in Old Forge," she said. "During the Depression, we traded to the neighbors, and, of course, we always made our own butter. There was always a 3-quart pitcher of milk on the table, and sometimes it had to be filled twice, and we would keep a pitcher of heavy cream out for poor man's dessert." Simpler times, simpler pleasures. Louise's poor man's dessert of bread, sugar, and heavy sweet cream could not be afforded by local gourmets at today's prices.

The large garden, animals, and traditional ingenuity served them well, and the traditional values were passed on to a new generation of Inlet residents.

The Paynes later owned a boat livery at Seventh Lake,

which Richard and Louise operated from 1946 until 1960. Louise was deeply involved in the business, renting cabins, running the store, administering the boats and gasoline sales, and helping with her husband's construction company. They left the business when Richard's health failed, and Louise still has many kind words for her experiences in the business community. "I enjoyed the business," she says adamantly. "I met very many nice people through the years."

*   *   *

Here follow a few short descriptions of some of Inlet's more memorable characters and their stories: Bill Bailey's claim to fame was his constant companion, the invisible dog, Hannibal. Everyone greeted the dog as well as the man whenever they met. Bill loved to be on the water, and after his motor boat, Chuckles, ran no more, he could be seen almost every morning rowing a guideboat briskly down the lake, accompanied, of course, by Hannibal.

*   *   *

A tragic story is told about Abner Blakeman, one of the early settlers:

> After dinner on October 14, 1925, Abner decided to go for a walk with his little granddaughter, Irene. They walked down to the Head [as everyone called the village of Inlet, it being at the head of the lake], and were going home by way of the Gilbert Road when the wind started to blow. At the top of the hill, about where the drive for the Community Church is, Joseph Payne stopped with his new car and asked them to get in and see it. He was about to shift gears and proceed to Gilbert Road when a sudden gust uprooted a tree. The tree fell across the car hitting Abner and caving in the front of his head. Irene was also hit, the tree crushing her skull and knocking out one eye. Joe blessedly was uninjured and went to get help. Abner and Irene were both unconscious. They were taken to the Blakeman home and each put into downstairs bedrooms. Neither of them regained consciousness. Neighbors and

family came to comfort and stand by the wounded and grieving, as was the custom. Irene died in the first hours of October 15, and Abner soon after at 6:30 A.M. They were buried in Sands Cemetery in Grieg, New York.

* * *

Many tragic accidents happened that were related to the weather. Henry Spencer froze to death in the woods while attempting to reach a hunting camp. Harry Meneilly was cutting across the ice on Fifth Lake to reach his home on the South Shore Road when he fell through the ice. Although rescued by Herman Williston and others who heard his shouts, he did not survive.

* * *

A humorous story is told about the couple who were walking to Inlet down the Tote Road (currently South Shore Road) to get a piece of glass for their outdoor toilet. The wife wanted a large window so she could see the view, the husband wanted a small window so no one could see in. They argued all the way. Finally they bought the big glass. On the way home, he tripped. So a small window was put in the toilet.

* * *

There is a fly story told by Dianne Thibado:

Henry and Hattie (Payne) Thibado were involved in the winter of family humor. After they were first married, but before any of the children came along, one day there was a housefly buzzing around the house, which was annoying Hattie to the point of fretting... so Henry told her, "Get my 22 and I'll shoot it." She fetched his 22 and he did. My father (Charles Thibado) laughs when he tells the tale, but says seriously, "My father was one of the finest marksmen I've ever seen."

* * *

Herman Williston was a rather interesting character. Born in Turin, he moved to Inlet in 1910. He operated the Inlet Supply Company for many years and cut hair on the porch or in the kitchen of his home, across from where the Inlet Marina is now, for 25 cents a clip. He moved into the woodshed at the request of the board of health or in response to the weather. In his house was an orchestra of instruments, including piano, violin, bass, guitar, and sax, all of which he enjoyed playing. He was married to Elizabeth Scullion. Their idea of a vacation was for each to go upstairs separately for two weeks.

* * *

When Bob Hall graduated from the Inlet Common School, Herb Williston gave him a pair of ankle spats. The gift card read, "You will always have these." Ironically, when the Hall home burned in 1959, these spats were found wrapped in the same brown paper they were received in, not touched by the fire which destroyed nearly everything else in the house.

* * *

Bob West is remembered for his walking tours. He walked to Utica on at least one occasion when he had business there and one day, feeling insulted by something that happened in Lake Pleasant, refused a ride home and walked all the way back to his house on the South Shore Road.

* * *

Joanne Vogan is a heroine in the story of a fire on the Gilbert Road. A young mother, living in the apartment above the garage next to Joanne's, left her two young children alone, as was her custom, while she went to the Post Office. One unfortunate day, fire broke out while she was gone, and the children would almost certainly have perished in it, if Joanne, seeing the fire and knowing the circumstances, had not rushed up to save them.

* * *

Then there is the story remembered by David Beetle in *The Utica Observer* in 1948:

> There was a certain amount of informality about conducting county affairs (especially in view of the County seat being so inaccessible). An Inlet constable who was supposed to take a couple of minor law-breakers around to the Hamilton County Jail, got as far as Remsen, sat them down to a hearty meal, paid the restaurant owner and walked out. "Shucks," he told folks, "I couldn't be bothered going way over to Lake Pleasant with those guys."

* * *

No one ever spoke of going to "Inlet." They were going to the "Head," which made perfect sense, because it was at the head of the lake, or they were going "Uptown," which made no sense at all, because no matter from what direction one enters Inlet, it necessitates going down a hill.

* * *

As I mentioned before, "visiting" or swapping stories was a popular way of passing the time. One such story involves an old guide, Frank Baker. His rich employer said he could have anything he wanted, but was surprised by Baker's request for twelve alarm clocks. There was much speculation around the town as to what he would do with them. Then one day in late winter, Gerald Kenwell hoofed it over to Baker's camp. There sat the twelve clocks, all in a row on a shelf by the bunk. "What's the idea of all the alarm clocks?" quizzed Kenwell.

"As you know, it gets a little cool up here sometimes, so when I go to bed, I set one for each hour of the night. In that way they wake me up every hour, and without getting up I reach over and stick some wood into the nearby stove. That way I am assured the fire won't go out. Them clocks have been a great help," Baker replied.

* * *

Bearded, lank and tall Lincoln Caswell could easily be mistaken for Abraham Lincoln had he lived in a different era. He, his daughter, whose flowing hair fell below her hips, and his rather small wife, who always seemed to wear black, came from New York City in the summer to rent their rather run-down cabins and cause heads to turn whenever they appeared in town.

* * *

Riley Johnston, who arrived in 1896, notes there was no road north of McKeever. He and his companion slept next to their bags of onions and potatoes to keep them from freezing.

* * *

I believe Gerald Kenwell was the guide who was asked by a hunter, "What was the most horrible sound you ever heard, the cry of a panther or the howl of a wolf?" "Neither," the old guide replied, "The worse sound I ever heard was the tin cup scraping the bottom of the flour barrel. That meant I had to go fifty-five miles over that damn road to get more flour."

* * *

There are two things that come to my mind when I think of differences between those days and now. The first is that even young girls never went "Uptown" without putting on a skirt. Although we were allowed to wear shorts around the house, we always covered them with a skirt if we were going out in public.

The other thing, that appalls me as I look back on it, is the fact that raw sewage emptied into the channel from the establishments along its shore. I often rowed to town and would see sewage pouring out from under the tree roots as I passed along.

* * *

Supposedly, just one person has the dubious honor of being buried in Inlet. Will Payne's final resting place is near the Inlet Golf Course, marked by a small white cross. But the confusion lies in the fact that on the list of Hamilton County Veterans of World War I, a man by the name of West is named as "the only one that died and was buried in Inlet."

Appendix A

Part 1
1900 Census—Town Of Morehouse

Kenwell, Wellington (41)   head
    Elizabeth (36)   wife
    Gerald (13)   son, at school
    Laura (8)   daughter, at school
    Louis Stevens(15)   chore boy
    Raymond Norton   employee, laborer

Hart, Henry (38)   carpenter
    Libbie B. (28)   wife
    George Burdick (26)   brother-in-law
    Jacob Hart (77)   father
    Lyle Hart (4)   son
    Carlton Hart (1)   son

Leach, Milo (36)   head, carpenter
    Elizabeth J. (32)   wife
    Timothy O'Barra (23)   boarder, boatman
    Richard Kelly (26)   boarder, day laborer

Hess, Frederick (53)   head, hotel keeper
    Ellen (48)   wife
    Robert D. Burton (24)   son-in-law, teamster
    Alice Burton (22)   daughter
    Laura J. Burton (72)   grand-daughter
    Sadie M. Claffy (20)   waitress
    Mamie Claffy (18)   waitress
    Lulu Marby (18)   waitress

Josephine Singer (24)	waitress
Charles Lamont (27)	employee, bartender
Frederick N. Kirch (26)	boarder, guide
Frank Loson (28)	boarder, day laborer

Moshier, William D. (43)	head, hotel keeper
Gertrude (27)	wife
Margery M. (2)	daughter
Nellie A. Sullivan (28)	servant

O'Hara Charles (29)	head, merchant-grocer
Caroline (29)	wife
Vernon B.(1)	son
Edward P. Murry (20)	employee, grocery clerk
Emma Munsey (23)	employee, waitress
Riley Johnston (23)	employee, mason

Van Arnam, Christopher (53)	head, mason
Josephine (48)	wife
Dora L. (13)	daughter, at school

Delmarsh, George (59)	head, post master
? (59)	wife
Archie G. (29)	son
Eri S. (19)	son
William B. Vanarnam (89)	father

Jones, Clinton H.	head, carpenter
? (29)	wife
? (4)	daughter

Tiffany, Frank (36)	head, painter
Anna (29)	wife
Lansing (3)	son
Laura Kirch (21)	sister-in-law, school teacher

Haines, Philip (51)	head, carpenter
Josephine (49)	wife
Timothy O'Barra (23)	boarder, boatman
Richard Kelly (26)	boarder, day laborer

(Note: O'Barra is listed under Leach as well)

Ward, John (62)   head, caretaker-Pratt estate
   Margaret (63)   wife
   Anna M. Forsberg (18)   employee, servant

Gallut? Egbert H. (53)   head, carpenter
   Mary J. (44)   wife
   Izzie (23)   daughter
   Charles L. (20)   son, day laborer
   Fred E. (14)   son, at school
   Mary E. (7)   daughter, at school
   Bert L. Hough (24)   son-in-law, day laborer

Brown, Albert E. (23)   head, school teacher
   Francie (26)   sister, at school
   Austin A. Dobson (35)   employee, machinist
   Nellie Dobson (35)   wife
   Harlow C. Hough (66)   employee, day laborer
   Charles Rieten (26)   employee, month laborer
   Wallace Jones (33)   employee, day laborer
   Joseph Nanetowich (30)   employee, partner to head

Woolslegger, Frederick (52)   head, sawyer in mill
   Julia (41)   wife

Blakeman, Abner (29)   head, guide
   Katie (29)   wife
   Flossie (8)   daughter
   Margeruitte (4)   daughter

Murdock, Allan (38)   head, carpenter
   Estella C. (32)   wife
   Donald (13)   son
   Claude R. (11)   son
   Una (5)   daughter
   Ina M. (3)   daughter
   Matteson (1/12)   son
   Bert P. (31)   brother, day laborer

Harwood,? (64)   head, day laborer
   Emmil (62)   wife

Murdock, Fred C. (32)	head, wheel wagoner
Lillian B. (29)	wife
Hazel (9)	daughter
Webb R. (7)	son
Ernest G. (5)	son
Frederick (3)	son
Lillian (11/12)	daughter
Frank D. (41)	brother, guide
Jessie M. (15)	niece, at school

Part 2
1910 Census—Town of Inlet

Bill, William E.   head, house painter
   Williston, Herman J. (28)   servant, musician
   Williston, Bertha L. (28)   wife, servant, musician
   Wood, Williard F. (67)   servant, musician

Peebles, John 31)   head, laborer, guide
   Laperic, Ned (54)   servant, laborer, teamster
   Bonifazie, James (19)   servant, laborer-common
   Brown, Asa (51)   laborer, gardener

Hart, Henry (48)   head, jobber, carpenter
   Elizabeth (38)   wife
   Lyle (14)   son
   Carlton (11)   son
   Burdick, Edward (24)   servant, laborer-common

Rarick, Arthur A.(41)   head, laborer, machinist
   Ella (32)   wife
   Catherine Ann (73)   mother

Leitch, Miloh (46)   head, laborer, guide
   Elizabeth (42)   wife

Davis, Henry (35)   head, laborer-common
   Sarah E. (28)   wife
   Grace A. (4)   daughter
   Freddie (3)   son
   Alice (2)   daughter

Rogers, Roy W. (28)   head, laborer-common
   Emma L. (32)   wife
   Beatrice J. (5)   daughter
   Ella I. (2)   daughter

Tiffany, Frank E. (46)   head, agent-real estate
   Anna K. (39)   wife

Lansing K. (13)   son

Burr, Peter (59)   head, carpenter
  Katherine E. (47)   wife
  Goldie (11)   daughter
  Frances (4)   daughter
  Milton (2)   son

Kirch, Charles D. (24)   head, laborer, guide
  Jennie M. (21)   wife
  Florence E. (112)   daughter

Delmarsh, Eri S. (29)   head, laborer, guide
  Bertha M. (24)   wife

Delmarsh, George (69)   head, retired
  Mary S. (66)   wife

Van Arnam, Christopher (63)   head, stonemason
  Josephine (58)   wife

VanArnam, Everett J. (34)   head, laborer, guide
  Florence (32)   wife
  Winifred (4)   daughter

O'Hara, Charles A. (38)   head, merchant-general store
  Carrie E. (39)   wife
  Rernar? (12)   son
  Alton (4)   son

Wilson, Hayden (37)   head, laborer, painter
  Charlotte, Mabel (26)   wife

Wood, Philo, C. (37)   head, hotel keeper
  Elizabeth (35)   wife
  Charles (15)   son
  Florence (19)   daughter
  Madeline (6)   daughter
  Marjoree (1)   daughter
  Wellington, George (74)   father-in-law
  Wellington, Elizabeth (63)   mother-in-law
  Wetmore, Ezera (42)   boarder, guide

Wetmore, Ella (38)	servant, pastry cook
Wetmore, Ethel (15)	boarder
Carroll, Nellie (34)	boarder, trained nurse
Burdick, Ethel (31)	servant, waitress
Dodge, Dr. George E. (37)	boarder, general physician
Warwick, Lou (27)	boarder (female)
Wilcox, Emmet ? (64)	servant, teamster
Beth? (33)	servant, waitress-hotel
Breakey, Samuel (26)	boarder, guide
Rubar?, Charles (36)	servant, laborer-common
Dayton, Robert (27)	servant, laborer-common
Gifford, Ernest (25	servant, machinist -stationary engine
Craver, William (24)	boarder, laborer
Murphy, Edward (22)	boarder, laborer, barber
Wellington, Joseph (39)	boarder, steamboat captain
Rarick, Edgar (30)	boarder, laborer, bridge worker
Rarick, George (24)	boarder, laborer, guide
Peebles, Howe (24)	servant, laborer, teamster
Conkling, George E. (35)	servant, laborer, blacksmith
Kennedy, Arthur (61)	servant, laborer-common
Hopkins, John (21)	boarder, laborer-common
Moore, Arthur D. (27)	
Williams, Frank A. (34)	head, hotel keeper
Jennie (36)	wife
Harold C. (11)	son
Lewis, Everett (25)	servant, laborer-common
Lewis, Bertha (26)	servant, waitress
Lewis, Robert (34)	servant, teamster
Fredette, Dominick (19)	servant, laborer-common
Fredette, Modest (20)	servant, laborer-common
McGarr, Eddie (34)	servant, laborer-common
Murdock, Una (15)	servant, waitress
Wemple, Olivia (46)	sister-in-law
Murphy, James (18)	servant, laborer-common
Cole, Elmer M. (49)	head, contractor-home builder
Eckler, James T. (45)	servant, carpenter
Eckler, Jennie E. (47)	servant, cook
Conway, George (40)	servant, carpenter
Collis(?), Frank (50)	servant, carpenter

Johnson, F.R. (33)   head, jobber-mason
   Rena (32)   wife
   Cecil (8)   son

Porter, Lewis (35)   head, carpenter-house
   Esther (27)   wife
   Rilla (8)   daughter
   Louise (6)   daughter
   Orrin (2)   son
   Thibado, Lizzie (16)   sister-in-law

Kenwell, Wellington (52)   head, merchant-supply
   Elizabeth (46)   wife
   Gilchrist, Christine (65) servant
   Patrick, William (23)   servant, laborer-common
   Paddock, Mason (?)(29) servant, teamster

Woolsleger, Fred (62)   head, guide
   Julia (52)   wife

Gilbert, Devine (37)   head, guide
   Virgie (23?)   wife
   Kenneth (14)   son

Richards, George D. (46)   head, foreman-mill
   Mary E. (45)   wife
   Walter (16)   son
   Nellie (14)   daughter
   George (8)   son

Trotter, Fred (37)   head, laborer-common
   Anna (36)   wife
   Daphne O. (22)   daughter
   Phyllis I. (112)   adopted daughter

Murdock, AC (48)   head, carpenter
   Estelle (42)   wife
   Inez (13)   daughter
   Matteson (9)   son
   Guy (5)   son
   Ralph (2)   son

Blakeman, Abner (39)	head, laborer, guide
Kate (39)	wife
Majorie (14)	daughter
George A. (9)	son
Rosa M. (5)	daughter
Retha (3)	daughter
George M. (63)	father
Cuming, John (29)	head, laborer-common
Mattie (29)	wife
Bertha A. (7)	daughter
Harold H. (5)	son
Bartlet H. (2)	son
Gilchrist, William (31)	head, laborer-common
Ella (36)	wife
Beyor, Michael (23)	boarder, laborer-common
Loson(?), Frank (44)	head, guide
Mercy (37)	wife
Elizabeth A. (6)	daughter
Raymond (37)	head, carpenter
Edith (36)	wife
Leland B. (32)	son
Gebhard, Mabel (38)	boarder, teacher
Burdick, Wright (39)	head
Alice (37)	wife
Anna (9)	daughter
Russell (7)	son
Rexford (5)	son
Vivian (82)	daughter
Horth, Rober L. (21)	head, laborer-common
Mabel (19)	wife
Ford, Albert P. (35)	head, laborer, guide
Mernie (25)	wife
Alice L. (3)	daughter
Gertrude (12)	daughter
Ford, Harry (27)	brother, laborer-common

Ford, Erwin (29)   head, teamster
   Nina (23)   wife

Rosa, Walter A. (35)   head, laborer-common
   Dora (33)   wife

Parquet, Fred N. (29)   head, post master
   Myrtle (25)   wife
   Thelma (1)   daughter

Thompson, William (59)   head, guide

Goodwin, James (50)   laborer, navigator
   Lela M. (40)   wife
   Mateline (12)   daughter
   Mary A. (10)   daughter

Buckingham, Joseph (41)   head, laborer

Cedar Island

Delmarsh, A.G. (39)   head, summer hotel landowner
  Laura K. (30)   wife
  Gaylord, Roy (23)   servant, laborer-common

Cascade Lake

Wells, Frank (44)   head, foreman
  Worstley, Raymond (35)   servant, farm laborer

Eagle Bay

Preston, Mrs. W.A. (39)   head, landlord-hotel
  Alfred (2)   son
  Tobin, Ella (29)   servant, assistant stenographer
  Tobin, Lizzie (28)   servant, domestic

Appendix B

Elected Officials

Supervisors

1902–1925	Frank E. Tiffany
1926–1931	Clarence E. Lee
1932–1962	K. Leonard Harwood
1962	Norton Bird

Town Clerks

1902–1905	Charles A. O'Hara
1906–1908	Everett J. Van Arnam
1909–1915	William E. Bill
1916–1918	D.C. Davis
1919	Florence Puffer

(Appointed on July 29, 1919, to fill vacancy.)

1920	William Craver
1921–1923	Ellwood J. Searles
1924–1925	Philip H. Jones
1926–1931	Harry H. Hall
1932–1941	Emmett Roberts
1942–1943	William H. Payne (died in office)
1943	Florence Turner Payne

(Appointed on August 19, 1943 to fill vacancy; resigned in November 1943)

1944–1953	Clinton Schaller

(Appointed to fill vacancy.)

1954–1957	Laura Bird
1958–1959	Bernard Patrick
1960–1961	Laura Bird
1962–1964	Alberta Dodd

Appendix C

Hamilton County Veterans of World War I

James Abusia
C. Roy Murdock
Eugene Cameron
Harrison Sawyer
Rev. F. Fehlner
Louis Snyder
Oscar Hall
Lansing Tiffany
Raymond Kopp

Arthur Lucas
Howard Burkard
Bernard O'Hara
Dr. F. S. Cole
Ellwood J. Searles
Kenneth Gilbert
Henry Thibado
Mark Kenville
Harold Williams

Issac Blair
Edward Murphy
John Clayton
Clinton Schaller
Modeste Fredette
Edwood Terry Berry
Lyle Hart
West*

Hamilton County Veterans of World War II

James Abusia
Evan Murdock
Edward Breen
Bernard Patrick
Richard Burnett
Robert Rasick

Robert Meneilly
George Blakeman Jr.
Arthur Patrick
William Breen Jr
Theodore P. Payne
Charles Cole

Donald Ball
Winfred Murdock
Elsie Breen
Richard Payne Jr.
Durcan Cameron

* The only one that died and was buried in Inlet

Appendix D

First Town Board Minutes—January 14, 1902

Minutes of a special town meeting of the Town of Inlet held at hotel of C. A. O'Hara, January 14, 1902. Polls opened 7:27 A.M. F. E. Tiffany, C. H. Jones, and C. A. O'Hara as a committee appointed by Board of Supervisors having charge of the meeting. C. A. O'Hara and C. H. Jones swear in and signed the necessary papers by F. E. Tiffany, Notary Public.

F. E. Tiffany sworn in by C. H. Jones, Justice of Peace. Polls closed at 5 o'clock P.M. Ballot box opened; number of ballots in the box was 35.
Box containing stubs offered and counted; number in same was 35.
The whole number of votes cast was 35, of which F. E. Tiffany,
  candidate for Supervisor, received 34.
C. A. O'Hara, candidate for Town Clerk, received 34.
  Term 4 years. December 31, 1905.
John F. Cassidy, candidate for Justice of Peace, received 34.
  Term 4 years. December 31, 1905.
Raymond Norton, candidate for Justice of Peace, received 34.
  Term 2 years. December 1902.
Christopher G. Van Arnam, candidate for Justice of Peace, received 34.
Austin A. Dobson, candidate for Assessor, received 34.
Fred N. Kirch, candidate for Commissioner of Highways, received 33.
W. Kenwell, candidate for Commissioner of Highways, received 1.
R. G. Wallace, candidate for Commissioner of Highways, received 34.
Peter Burr, Candidate for Collector, received 34.
William Wilkinson, candidate for Constables, received 34.
Frank Stahl, candidate for Constables, received 34.
Abner Blakeman, candidate for Game Constable, received 34.
Blank Ballots, 1.

Nominations for above officers are from Democrat and Republican parties. It being a union meeting.

Bibliography

Aber, Ted and Stella King. *The History of Hamilton County.*
Great Wilderness Books: Lake Pleasant, NY, 1965.

Beetle, David. *Up Old Forge Way.* North Country Books:
Utica, NY 1984.

Burnap, W. Donald. *Heartwood.* The Brown Newspapers:
Baldwinsville, NY, 1988.

Longstaff, George. *From Heyday to Mayday.* Valkyrie Publishing
House: St. Petersburg, FL, 1983.

About the Author

Letty Kirch Haynes was born and grew up in Watertown, New York. After high school, she went to the University of Rochester and graduated with a degree in Sociology. Returning to Watertown, she worked as a case worker in the children's division of the Jefferson County Welfare Department.

After a wonderful trip to Europe with two friends, she met her husband back in Watertown. His work as Claims Manager for Traveler's Insurance took them first to Westvale in Syracuse, then to Maine, and finally to Massachusetts. Wherever they lived, they always managed to spend their summers in the Adirondacks. They had four children, two surprising them as twins.

While in Syracuse, Letty started taking courses necessary for a degree in elementary school teaching, which she began to do in Maine. Upon semi-retirement, they moved full time to Letty's grandfather's old home on Fourth Lake, and she taught in the Inlet Common School for twenty years, enjoying very much the little four room school with two classes in every room, no cafeteria or gym, but high academic achievement due in part to the small class sizes. Letty still substitute teaches there whenever she can.

After nearly fifty-two years of marriage, Letty lost her husband, but she continues to be thankful for the beautiful place in the Adirondacks where she is privileged to live.